The Beguiling Serpent

A Re-evaluation of Emotions and Values

Comment on earlier work by Hunter Lewis:

"Helps students. . . in actual human decision-making."

> —HARVEY COX, professor of divinity, Harvard University, author of *Many Mansions* and *The Secular City*

"Helps to make sense of. . . the diversity of values in our society."

> —PATRICIA H. WERHANE, Senior Fellow, Olsson Center for Applied Ethics, The Darden School, University of Virginia

"Lucid writing lets the reader share. . . insights on an intimate, one-to-one basis."

> —SAMUEL L. HAYES III, Jacob Schiff Professor of Investment Banking, Harvard Business School

"Enormously worthwhile. . . provides a unique way of organizing our thinking about values."

> —ADELE SIMMONS, president, MacArthur Foundation

"Brilliant work on what is by far the most important topic in modern politics, philosophy, economics, and psychology—namely, values."

> —KEN WILBUR, editor, *New Science Library*, and author of *Transformation of Consciousness*

"Stimulating. . . an eye opener."

> —DOROTHY R. and HOMER A. THOMPSON, Institute for Advanced Study, Princeton, New Jersey

The Beguiling Serpent

A Re-evaluation of
Emotions and Values

Hunter Lewis

Axios Press

Axios Press
PO Box 118
Mount Jackson, VA 22842

888·542·9467   press@axiosinstitute.org

Library of Congress Catalog Card Number: 00-101201
ISBN: 096619084X

A word about this book's title:

The emotional portion of the human brain has sometimes been described, not accurately but picturesquely, as the reptilian brain. On this level, the serpent of the title is simply a metaphor for our emotions.

This serpent, however, is beguiling, which refers to the story of the Garden of Eden as told in the King James translation of the Bible. The encounter with the serpent in the first book of the Bible is portrayed as the first value judgment that human beings make, indeed a value judgment that opens up the entire realm of "good and evil" for people to sort out. In the context of Genesis, of course, "good and evil" have specific religious connotations involving the concept of sin. By contrast, this book is concerned with the interplay of emotion with all our value judgments, not only value judgments about good and evil, but also about good and bad, just and unjust, beautiful and ugly, and innumerable variations and gradations including all the smaller value judgments that each of us must make on a daily basis.

Contents

Introduction

In his autobiography, *Naturalist*, leading evolutionary biologist Edward O. Wilson described how (later Nobel laureate) James Watson "arrived at Harvard with a conviction that biology must be transformed into a science directed at molecules and cells and rewritten in the language of physics and chemistry. What had gone before, traditional biology—*my* biology—was infested by stamp collectors who lacked the wit . . . [for] modern science . . . ."[1]

Watson's successors, in method if not in attitude, have made major advances in unraveling the mysteries of the human body but have proceeded haltingly with respect to the brain, and even more haltingly with respect to the emotions. In part, this is because it is so difficult to experiment on human beings—the tools employed, even in the era of the P.E.T. scan and M.R.I. and advanced laboratories, are still primitive, especially when compared to what they may become as bio-technology advances. But even with the best tools, a further and even more basic obstacle exists: when we move our emotional brains off the couch and into the laboratory, it is not all clear what we are looking for, what we would like to prove or disprove.

Dr. William R. Uttal captured this basic dilemma in his 1978 text, *The Psychobiology of Mind*: " . . . In light of the totally inadequate taxonomy of mental process and behaviors, which is, perhaps, more blatant in the field of emotion than in any other area of psychology, it may be that many of the questions we are asking in the psychobiological laboratory are not only unanswered but also essentially meaningless."[2] Dr. Robert Zajonc of the University of Michigan continued in a similar vein in 1993: "What we call certain emotions—sadness, fear, rage, anger and so on—do not correspond to specific patterns within the brain. Just like you cannot find in the brain who is a Democrat or who is a Republican."[3] Under these circumstances, it is hardly surprising that neurobiologist Dr. James McGaugh of the University of California in Irvine observed in 1996 that "emotions are not a dominant theme in neuroscience" and his colleague Dr. Michael Gazzaniga of Dartmouth College added that many scientists have simply assumed that it might prove "impossible [to understand] the neuroanatomy of emotions."[4] As if to reinforce this generally skeptical attitude, researchers in 1993 published a review (meta-analysis) of twenty-two separate studies of various antidepressant medications that represented the first (and much ballyhooed) attempt to control emotions biochemically, and concluded that such medications were barely better than a placebo (sugar pill) and often highly toxic and dangerous as well.[5]

In 1996, Dr. Joseph LeDoux of New York University seemed to cut through all the (unmistakably emotional) gloom about the scientific study of emotions with the publication of his book, *The Emotional Brain*. As Dr. LeDoux said:

"I was naïve enough to think that emotions could be studied"[6]; and he proceeded to establish a scientific definition of a particular emotion, fear, and to trace its neuroanatomy in rats, thereby conclusively proving that at least one emotion could be studied as a purely biological phenomenon. Even Dr. LeDoux's groundbreaking work, however, left many important questions unanswered. If one emotion, fear, has been shown to have an understandable physiological basis in rats, and inferentially in humans, are other emotions equally universal and basic to our physical being? If so, what are these emotions? How can they be defined, differentiated, studied? How do they interact with each other? How do they interact with the rest of our mind? What does all this mean for emotional therapies? And perhaps most importantly, what is the relationship between universal and basic emotions and our values, especially our emotional values, the personal attitudes, preferences, and beliefs that shape our lives?

All the doubts, all the cautious statements by respected scientists ("we have got as far as we will [in the study of the brain])"[7] notwithstanding, I still think there is no reason to be pessimistic, no reason to assume that many of these questions cannot be answered in a laboratory as the tools improve. In expressing this personal opinion, it is not my intention to join the "reductionists"— that is, those people who adopt the essentially metaphysical view that *all* mental processes can be "reduced" to biochemistry. Nor do I think that the management of the emotions will someday simply be a matter of popping the right pill. Rather, the main point I wish to make here is different. It is that even when the tools do improve, even when the techniques for identifying emotional pathways, both cellular and molecular, with related biochemical processes and markers, do become much more advanced than today, we will still need hunches, hypotheses, theories for the new tools and techniques to test and, through testing, either to prove or disprove.

This book presents one such hunch or hypothesis that will someday, when the tools are better, be at least partly testable and thus either largely confirmed or discarded. I should emphasize that this book is not itself intended to be a work of science. It is not even an example of the kind of clinical or empirical psychology that at least seems more scientific. It is rather something quite old-fashioned: a work of speculative psychology, the sort of thing that psychologists did when they were considered philosophers rather than scientists. At the same time, there is always a role for speculative psychology, perhaps especially today. Science cannot get started without hypotheses to test, and from this point of view, the broader and bolder the hypotheses the better.

I should also emphasize that not everything in this book will be even partly testable, not even when the tools are much better. Part of the hypothesis presented here about emotions and values and their interaction takes the form of terminology, a way of describing things that will not be testable per se, but will rather prove to be convenient or not convenient, a useful way of organizing and remembering ideas or not. Even so, I hope and expect that at least the central thesis of this book about the nature and number of emotions, and perhaps more, will eventually be verifiable by biochemical means.

So what is the central thesis of this book, and why should a reader devote his or her limited time to it, apart from satisfying curiosity about how emotions (and thus human beings) really work? This is a fair question for any author, one that deserves an honest but above all a brief answer. First of all, the central thesis of this book is that each of us has five (and only five) universal and basic emotions, not an infinite number as some psychologists believe, nor ten or more as perhaps most psychologists believe today. These five universal and basic emotions (which can be summarized, behaviorally, as grabbing, fleeing, fighting, giving up, or enjoying) not only guide our immediate responses in life, but also become elaborated into complete value systems underlying all our choices.

The notion of having a finite number of universal and basic emotions—in this case five— has some very important consequences, both scientifically and personally. On a scientific level, we must be able to define, identify, and number emotions, or we will not be able to look for them in our body, principally through blood work. If we cannot look for emotions inside the body, we will not be able to provide conclusive diagnoses of emotional problems. If we lack conclusive diagnoses of emotional problems, of emotions gone awry, we will have much more difficulty developing treatments, whether those treatments involve drugs or counseling.

For example, at the present time, twenty percent of all Americans are believed to suffer from one emotional disorder or another, including (from largest numbers to lowest) anxiety, phobias, substance abuse, depression, obsessive compulsion, cognitive impairment, schizophrenia, and anti-social personality. Both patients and doctors are forced to guess about the applicability of these emotional labels. The patient tries to capture in words how he or she feels, the doctor replies in words, a drug may also be selected and tried, the patient and doctor again express their subjective reactions in words about what has happened. Without a reliable blood test, it is impossible to be sure whether the patient has responded. To get beyond this still primitive stage, where the doctor still functions to some extent as a shaman, to get to the point where emotions really do come off the couch and into the laboratory, we must hypothesize that there are some universal, basic, physiologically detectable emotions, and we must start by hypothesizing what they are.

The idea of five universal and basic emotions is potentially most important on a scientific level but can be turned to immediate, personal use as well. Although this book is not primarily intended as a self-help guide, especially of the uplifting or exhortatory kind, one can and should use the idea of the five basic emotions and their elaboration into emotional value systems to monitor and manage one's own emotions. Because the scheme of the five emotions is so simple, so easy to remember, it provides a ready framework within which to observe one's own emotions, and the observing, if practiced often enough, becomes a kind of therapy.

Like all therapies, this one is more complicated than it seems and will be more reliable for some people than for others. The reason is that therapies are not, indeed cannot be, the objective, even quasi-scientific tools that we would like them to be, and this is just as true for drug-based as for talk-based techniques. Therapies are actually and inescapably embodiments and expressions of particular value systems; when we "shop" for therapies, whether we know it or not, we are actually "shopping" for value systems.

A corollary and consequence of this is that the effectiveness of any therapy depends on the fit with an individual's own preexisting values, especially his or her own preexisting emotional values, a theme that is further explored in chapters nine and ten, which analyze conventional therapies in terms of the value systems they are "selling" either overtly or surreptitiously. For example, in the case of the fairly rudimentary therapeutic tool of self-observation, it should be obvious that people whose emotional difficulties lead them in the direction of being aloof from others, whether from fright or hurt, will find it easier to observe themselves than people who are chronically angry. And people whose nonemotional values lead them to admire the basic scientific tools of experiment and logic will find self-observation even more congenial. But regardless of one's orientation, a map of emotions, emotional values, and the myriad therapies that express these values is in some sense a map of one's own life's possibilities, and it is all the better if it can be used for personal as well as for scientific explorations.

Part One

EMOTIONS

1. Basic Emotions

❧ Given the number of words written about the emotions over the past century and the often intense obsessiveness with which advice has been rendered and "cures" sought, it is surprising how few full-scale theories have been proposed. There is of course Freud's, which—although largely discarded—still dominates in a way, precisely because it is a complete theory. If we are searching for a similarly complete paradigm today, a paradigm which tells us how emotions operate, whether they are infinite or finite, if finite, how many and how defined, there are relatively few candidates, although the work of psychologist Silvan Tomkins and his successors and colleagues comes closest in both scope and impact.

Tomkins, Izard, and Horney

In his seminal 1962 book, *Affect, Imagery, Consciousness*,[1] Tomkins introduced his concept of fundamental emotions, emotions that may take many forms but which underlie our entire emotional life. Twenty-nine years later, Carroll Izard of the University of Delaware, after years of collaboration with Tompkins and others,[2] published a definitive list of ten such fundamental emotions: interest/excitement, enjoyment/joy, sadness, anger, disgust and contempt, fear and anxiety, shyness, shame, guilt, and love. Izard and his colleagues refined this list from several thousand possibilities: for example, there are at least 1,780 words describing emotions in *Webster's Collegiate*, an abridged dictionary[3]* and 164 broad emotional word categories in *Roget's Thesaurus*.[4] Moreover, they took special care to check the list against facial expressions and other physical evidence, although they did not look inside the body to try to establish biochemical markers for the emotions cited.

At first glance, Izard's ten emotions appear to present a series of logical problems. In order to be rated fundamental or basic, an emotion should presumably meet several simple standards. First, it would seem reasonable to expect that a basic emotion should be easily distinguishable, not easily confused with other emotions; yet shame, guilt—and under some circumstances, shyness— share a common theme of self-criticism or self-abnegation.† Second, one would expect that a basic emotion should "affect" us deeply, yet

---

* The same word may appear in noun, verb, adjective, or adverb form but has been counted only once. Another dictionary study (A. F. C. Wallace and M. T. Carson, *Ethos* 1 (1973): pp.1–29) found over 2,000 words describing emotions. Not all emotions, of course, can be counted in this way. Emotions described by single words such as "love" are there. Emotions described by phrases such as "love of money" or "desire to be loved" are not. In addition, words that do not specifically describe emotions often become loaded with emotional connotations. For example, the phrase "South Sea Islands" connotes a feeling of emotional escape from civilization and its demands.

† In earlier writings, Izard sometimes combined shame and shyness as one category or, alternately, separated disgust and contempt. Love is also a more recent addition to the list.

interest and shyness seem much less affecting than anger or fear, both of which can turn human beings and societies upside down and lead directly to war and other calamitous events. Third, it would be surprising if a truly basic emotion did not evoke a strong and predictable behavioral response such as fear: avoid, or anger: attack, but by this standard both interest and excitement seem to fall short.

If Izard's list could be pared further, which of the ten might be most basic? In order to answer this question, we might take a hint from an especially acute observer of human beings in the twentieth century, psychiatrist Karen Horney. In her capstone work, *Human Growth and Neurosis*, Horney described three coping strategies commonly used by people: aggression, avoidance, and dependency. Although Horney did not explicitly say so, these strategies seem to reflect underlying emotions of anger, fear, and sadness. By adding a fourth emotional category of happiness (Horney left it out because she was writing about unhappy people), we would then arrive at a list of only four basic human emotions. This approach has been popularized by best-selling author Melodie Beattie in *Codependent No More*: "some therapists have cut the list [of basic emotions] to four: mad, sad, glad, and scared. These four [are] primary . . . , and all the rest . . . shades and variations."[5]

Five basic emotions

What we might refer to as the Horney model has the considerable merit of being both clear and simple. The question remains: Is it complete?* Is some emotion left out, some basic emotion that cannot or should not be dismissed as merely an aspect of or a variation on anger, fear, sadness, and happiness, perhaps even an emotion that has been missed in Tomkins' and Izard's somewhat longer lists of emotions?

In order to answer this, we need to consider briefly the special role that emotions appear to play in our lives. In evolutionary and biological terms, what we commonly refer to as emotions are simply those more primitive elements of our brain that scan the environment and take especially strong command whenever an event seems threatening or otherwise urgent. Among higher animals as well as humans, emotions are highly reactive, modulating our energy level and if necessary propelling us into a very specific action such as "fight," "flight," or "capitulation," and also highly social, generally regulating our relations with other creatures.

Imagine, therefore, that you are alone by the shore of an isolated lake in an unfamiliar forest on a gentle summer day and suddenly confront a stranger. What emotional reaction do you have? If the stranger walks up and takes a swing at your head, you will presumably feel anger. If he or she points a gun at you, you will presumably feel fear. If the stranger turns out to be an enemy soldier who takes you captive, you will feel depressed as well as angry or fearful. If the stranger turns out to be a fellow bird watcher or has something else

---

* Even models of the emotions, perhaps especially models of the emotions, must be logical if they are to be potentially useful, and to be logical means, at a minimum, to be orderly, organized, internally consistent, clear, relevant and complete.

in common with you, you may feel pleased to make a new friend. In other words, you may be any of angry, fearful, sad, or happy.

But imagine further that it is a pleasantly warm day, that you decide to strip off your clothes to take a swim, that on rounding a bend, you discover a similarly unclothed stranger of pleasing form who is gracefully gliding through the water toward you. In this instance, you will presumably not feel anger or fear or sadness. You may well feel happy, but not in any sense of emotional balance or equilibrium, certainly not in any sense of quiet contentment. On the contrary, one will presumably feel aroused, in this case by sexual desire. Nor need desire always be sexually charged. An infant determined to be lifted into her mother's arms or breast fed or maniacally swiping a playmate's toy is exhibiting a presumptively nonsexual form of desire, albeit one that can be just as intense. So, at least provisionally, we might add a fifth major emotion, what might broadly be called desire, to the previously defined emotions of anger, fear, sadness, and happiness. Having done so, we now have five basic emotions which correspond to—and probably give rise to—the five most basic and primitive actions that we take in response to events in the world around us, a world comprised mostly of other creatures:

desire	$\rightarrow$	take, seize or grab;
fear	$\rightarrow$	avoid, flee;
anger	$\rightarrow$	attack, fight;
sadness	$\rightarrow$	give up, surrender, or capitulate;
happiness	$\rightarrow$	"live and let live."

Moreover, we may now begin to classify all emotive words as aspects of, or variations on, the basic five—aspects or variations that arise as our "higher" brain, no longer content to live solely in the very primitive world of the basic emotions, begins to experience, interpret, describe, embellish, and elaborate on these basic emotions. In other words, we "feel" the basic five, and only the basic five, but our sophisticated higher brain interprets these feelings in much more varied and nuanced ways (for example, we "feel" fear, but our higher brain may under certain circumstances interpret and elaborate on this as anxiety, panic, or mistrust):

The Basic Emotion	Words that Describe Aspects of or Variations on the Basic Emotion	Correlated at the Most Primitive Level with these Actions
desire	ambitious, demanding, willful	taking, seizing or grabbing
fear	anxious, mistrustful, panicked	avoiding or fleeing
anger	hostile, hypercritical, impatient	attacking or fighting
sadness	depressed, ashamed, hopeless	giving up, surrendering, or capitulation
happiness	calm, cheerful, pleased	"living and letting live"

Emotional disturbance and the five basic emotions

Throughout human history, emotional disturbance has been described in a great variety of ways, usually very complicated and often very fanciful ways. But, with the five basic emotions in mind, emotional disturbance can be defined in the simplest possible terms—as a general tendency to lapse too readily, or delve too deeply, or to linger too long, in emotional states of desire, fear, anger, or sadness.

These particular emotional states, it must be emphasized, are an absolutely necessary and normal part of life. From time to time we must all feel desire, fear, anger, or sadness in order to produce, on an immediate response basis and with as little conscious thought as possible, such adaptive behaviors as acquisitiveness, avoidance, aggression, or submission. On reflection, no matter how unimportant some of these sound, any of them may be needed for physical survival in a sometimes harsh world. The importance of having the emotional energy to get what we need and to flee from what threatens us is most obvious. But sometimes fighting is a better strategy for survival than fleeing and the arousal of anger makes us much better fighters. Conversely, if we are confronted with overpowering force, surrender may be best. Or on a somewhat subtler level, if we are too carried away with getting or fleeing or fighting, we may also need to be stopped "dead" in our tracks by the withdrawal of energy, the giving up, that comes with sadness.

Nor do we need these adaptive behaviors any less in the modern world. Without internal resources of aggression, we would be at the mercy of a Hitler or a Stalin, and there will always be potential Hitlers or Stalins. Without an ability to retreat and avoid everyday life, we could not, among other things, write books. Without the pain of sadness or momentary depression, we might not reassess and redirect our lives. Without the spur of desire, we might not even reproduce ourselves biologically.

Sometimes we have virtually no choice about our emotional state for a very long period of time. For example, British journalist John McCarthy, abducted from a car on the streets of Beirut and kept manacled to a wall throughout his captivity, reported soon after his release that: "Over the past few weeks I have been learning to relax again. It wasn't until a few days after my release that I realized that I hadn't in fact had any true peace of mind for over five years. A hostage doesn't relax."[6] In other words, although a hostage must try to repress some of his or her basic emotions (for example by not falling into an immobilizing depression or into dangerous anger), it is necessary and adaptive to remain fearful and anxiously alert at all times.

Many people, of course, live for long periods of time in anger or fear or sadness or unrestrained desire, and very few of them have been held physically captive. If the majority can be said to be held captive, it is by forces much more elusive than ordinary kidnappers, as we shall discuss further in Chapter Five.

For the moment, then, we are left with five basic emotions, no fewer, and a tendency either to fall into the first four emotional states unnecessarily, or exaggeratedly, or to linger in these states longer than absolutely necessary, as per the chart on the following page:

FIFTH EMOTION:

• Emotional states related to **happiness**, expressed as calm, cheer, balance, enjoyment, appreciation

• In behavioral terms, predisposed to "live and let live" or, better, to connect with people, activities, or objects

FOURTH EMOTION:

• Emotional states related to **sadness**

• In behavioral terms, predisposed to giving up, passivity, dependence, or submission; greatest good: being assisted or taken care of; greatest risk: masochism

FIRST EMOTION:

• Emotional states related to **desire**

• In behavioral terms, predisposed to taking, seizing, grabbing, demanding, bossing; greatest good: possessing X, Y, or Z; greatest risk: addiction

THIRD EMOTION:

• Emotional states related to **anger**

• In behavioral terms, predisposed to fighting, attacking, scorning, blaming; greatest good: dominance, revenge; greatest risk: sadism

SECOND EMOTION:

• Emotional states related to **fear**

• In behavioral terms, predisposed to avoidance, flight, nervousness; greatest good: independence; greatest risk: isolation

2. Shifting Emotions

🔥 So far we have presented a brief sketch of each of the first four basic emotions—desire, fear, anger, sadness—as if that emotion existed in isolation. This was a useful fiction, one that allowed us to focus on one emotion at a time, but far from an accurate description of human affairs. In actuality, we pass rapidly from one basic emotion to another and, even though they are all hypothesized to be biochemically distinct, they are still highly interrelated.

It is true that people very often develop a decided preference for one emotion over another. In a family, the oldest child may have barely controllable desires, up to or over the edge of some kind of serious addiction, and the next child may be fearful and withdrawn to the point of complete social isolation. But no matter how dominant a particular emotion may seem at a given moment or in a particular context or relationship, all the basic emotions will be in play to some degree, because they continually and inevitably interact with one another. In real life, an individual may simultaneously exhibit a demanding bossiness or angry sadism with an employee, a sadly spiritless and childish dependence with a parent, a trembling terror with an authority figure such as the police, and a greedy acquisitiveness with respect to money or power.

Even if one's emotional life is seemingly stable and consistent, it is difficult to stay in any one basic emotion for an extended period of time. A man may long for a particular automobile, which longing exemplifies desire. If he fails to get it, he may become angry that he is unable to afford it, or depressed that he is unable to afford it, or fearful that he will never be able to afford it, or he may feel all four emotions over and over in succession. Even if the man is able to make the purchase, he may still respond angrily that it cost so much, sadly that he will now have to give up some other purchase, or fearfully that it may cost too much to replace in the future. Moreover, people move between emotions so rapidly that the edges become blurred and responses garbled. As psychologist William James correctly observed at the beginning of the twentieth century, "Most cases are mixed cases."[1]

Confusion caused by shifting emotions

Precisely because we are always shifting emotional gears, sometimes quite rapidly, it is very easy to become confused about what is happening. It may seem that emotions are indistinguishable or interchangeable (e.g., Shakespeare's "To be furious is to be frighted out of fear").[2] Or it may seem that all emotions are really one, either because one emotion is more vivid (e.g. the angry bully) or because of the recurring human tendency to want to simplify. Thus some psychoanalysts have argued that depression should be viewed simply as repressed anger or anger against the self (according to this interpretation, anger is the key, underlying, unifying emotion).

Therapist John Bradshaw has suggested that all emotional problems may be reduced to shame (an emotion we have viewed as one aspect— although a particularly painful one—of sadness, because of its ability to rob us of energy and shut us down)   and that we can regain emotional health by learning not to be ashamed of ourselves. Albert Ellis, the inventor of rational emotive therapy, teaches that virtually all feelings of what we call emotional disturbance stem from "musturbation,"[3] that is, allowing our desires to convince us that everything should, ought, or must be a certain way. Similarly, therapist Ken Keyes, following the Buddhist tradition, suggested that most emotional discomfort could be overcome by redefining personal demands (desires) as preferences.

Ironically, there is a sense in which Bradshaw, Ellis, Keyes, and others are entirely correct. The basic emotions are so closely connected that people may free themselves from a chronic involvement in one emotion by working on a different one. Hence, even if individual X appears to be, most of all, chronically angry, if X works on the accompanying demanding, fear, or shame, he or she will probably reduce the chronic anger. This is not unlike the approach that a physical therapist may take with a tensed or spasmodic back muscle. The therapist may not start working or kneading the muscle spasm, but instead try to massage and relax other body muscles first, after which the muscle spasm will usually relax more readily. On the other hand, just because an approach of trying to turn demands into preferences works well in reducing fear and anger and shame as well as demands, this does not mean that all emotional disturbance can be reduced to demanding. Indeed, one can just as easily start the other way, by reducing one's anger or fear, and in the process one's demands will be quieted as well.

Paradoxes related to shifting emotions

The same tendency to confuse emotional states because they are closely connected may also help explain some of the paradoxes of recent drug research. Supporters of what might be called the "unified" view of the emotions argue that if antidepressants work on anger and fear as well as on sadness, surely we are dealing with a single underlying emotion, probably one best characterized as depression. But this is only one way to interpret the physical evidence and not necessarily the most likely one. The alternative explanation is that because the patient is continually passing through all four emotions, and because the four emotions are so highly interrelated, drugs that help relieve any of the four principal symptoms (unrestrained desire, fear, anger, or sadness) will help all of the symptoms, and thus help the patient, no matter what the principal symptom may be.

The rapidity with which we shift from one mood to another has created a second confusion as well: that each observable emotion is best thought of as a mask covering up some other, quite different, perhaps even opposite, emotion. The psychologist Karl Jung especially emphasized this idea: if someone seems very aggressive, it is to compensate for an underlying problem of timidity. If someone seems timid, it is to compensate for an underlying problem of aggressiveness. A great deal of psychological literature is full of this kind of paradoxism: patient A, suffering from disorder B, is extremely irresponsible, but this may manifest itself either in extreme irresponsibility or in extreme responsibility. Patient C, suffering from disorder D, is emotionally immobilized, but this may manifest itself either in immobility or in hyperactivity. Patient E, suffering from disorder F, is basically gentle, but there is a chance that this may manifest itself in murderous violence, etc., etc.

Even psychiatrist Karen Horney, usually so clear in her thinking, lapsed into this kind of confusing and circular analysis in her comment that "Compulsive drives are . . . born of feelings of isolation, helplessness, fear and hostility, and represent ways of coping with the world despite these feelings; they aim primarily not at satisfaction but at safety."[4] Although it is true that all these emotions constantly overlap and intermingle, there is no evidence that compulsive drives (seen here as an aspect of and especially strong variation on desire) are "born" in sadness, fear, or anger any more than sadness, fear, or anger are "born" in compulsive drives; nor is the statement "drives for satisfaction are really drives for safety" necessarily any more true than the obverse statement "drives for safety are really drives for satisfaction."

Unscrambling confusion and parodox

Fortunately there is a way to unscramble all this confusion, paradox, and contradiction. One simply recognizes that every person, not just a psychiatric patient, goes through unrestrained desiring, fearful, angry, and sad phases and that his or her attitudes and especially his or her behavior change accordingly. Thus a person who claims that he or she is Jesus Christ or Napoleon when in the throes of a mania will undoubtedly at some point shift back into sadness and morosely complain that he or she is a nobody. Similarly, an extremely aggressive person living frequently and deeply in anger, for example a mugger or other street criminal, will undoubtedly have moments of panic or terror in which all aggression is temporarily stripped away. Although the exact timing of these shifts is difficult to predict, it is possible to say with certainty that everyone will cycle through each of the major emotions in turn, and that his or her thoughts and behavior will reflect the emotion of the moment. For example, emotion-related thoughts typically include: "I demand X, cannot live without it, and have every right to boss myself and others to get it" [desire]; "I worry that I will die if I enter this airplane and/or I will 'die' from wounded pride if people think badly of me or if I think badly of myself" [fear]; "people and/or the world are unfair to me and I have every right to blame them/it" [anger]; "I have lost something forever and/or feel guilty because I have made unforgiveable mistakes" [sadness]). Commonly, these thoughts roll in one after another.

Nor is this continual mood-shifting a matter of opposites, of moving from point A to its obverse point B, as Jung and others thought. Our tendency to think in terms of dialectically opposed pairs such as justice and injustice or black and white arises in the logical portion of our mind and is often quite useful. But this particular kind of logical thinking does not fit the emotions. Although we commonly refer to manic-depression, in which a person is thought to alternate between manic desire and an opposing deeply sad depression, mania (in which wants become elevated to wildly unrealistic levels, often followed in quick succession by frustrated anger at anyone who seems to disagree or stand in the way) and depression (lacking the energy to want anything or even to be angry) are not any more opposite than mania and fear (avoiding or fleeing). Similarly, fear is just as much an opposite of anger (attacking or fighting) as it is of mania.

It is possible to pair off *groups* of basic emotions. Thus in general desire and fear tend to be more forward looking, more focused on the future, while in general anger and sadness tend to be more backward looking, more focused on the past. On the other hand, one could just as reasonably take the opposite tack of grouping fear and sadness together, because people living deeply in these emotions are generally aware that they are fearful or depressed, and consequently more timid, while people living deeply in desire or anger are often completely unaware that they are gripped by mania or anger, and consequently more aggressive. Similarly, one could speak of desire and anger as generally more active and fear and sadness as generally more passive, but a particular angry or demanding type (e.g., a "passive-aggressive") may be quite passive, while a particular fearful or sad type (e.g., an "escapist" or "martyr") may be quite active. On balance, therefore, it is not accurate or particularly useful to speak of any one major emotion as the so-called opposite of another.

Further complications

Perhaps the most confusing aspect of emotions is that, as we experience them, we may be experiencing emotions about others or about ourselves or about others and ourselves in quick succession. For example, in the midst of arguing with a spouse, we may be angry at the spouse, but also disappointed (sad) that we are handling the conflict poorly. As previously suggested, emotions seem to be highly reactive, modulating our energy and propelling us toward some specific action such as taking (desire), fleeing (fear), fighting (anger), or lack of action such as giving up (sadness), and generally regulating our relations with other creatures. The irony of human emotion, as opposed to most animal emotion, is that our self-consciousness, our ability to look at ourselves from the outside as if we were another creature (and not just to externalize ourselves but to evaluate and rate ourselves), adds an entire new layer of complexity to our emotional lives, opens up all sorts of opportunities for emotional misfiring by making it possible to turn our desire, fear, anger, or sadness on ourselves.

Among the early Christian Church fathers, Saint Augustine held that the root of all human suffering lay in original sin, the bite of the apple by Adam and Eve that led to self-consciousness. Julian the Apostate disagreed: suffering is an inescapable part of human life with or without self-consciousness. From today's perspective, one might conclude that both were right: baboons suffer from deranged emotional systems just as humans do, but conscious and especially self-conscious humans have the potential to suffer more. Both baboons and humans must make decisions every day that will determine the future direction their lives take. Neither baboons nor humans will make the best choice every time or even much of the time. But only humans must learn to live with their past mistakes and with the likelihood that each day will bring more of them. Nor do baboons have to worry about their emotions feeding on themselves as in becoming fearful of being afraid, angry about being depressed, or just more depressed about being depressed, with all the familiar physical accompaniments of sweaty palms, rapid heart beats, and sore back muscles that cannot heal because we cannot stop thinking about them. Nor are baboons self-conscious enough to want to hide behind masks, pretend that they are happy when actually angry, be sexually responsive when desire is at low ebb, or engage in some other minor or major emotional mendacity.

But whatever the case, whether people are being emotionally open, emotionally mendacious, mendacious about being open, open about being mendacious, or mendacious but in denial about being mendacious, the main point to keep in mind is that we always maintain an inner emotional dialogue with ourselves as if we are dealing with another person, with the result that any emotional strategy we use in our relations with others can also, and equally, be used to regulate relations with ourselves. Thus, we can be angry and abusive with others or with ourselves, demanding and manipulative with others or with ourselves, avoidant and reclusive out of fear of what others may come to think of us or out of fear of what we may come to think of ourselves, a chronically sad "defendant" in the harsh court of self-appraisal because of suffering we feel we have brought on others or because of suffering we feel we have brought on ourselves.

In thinking about this, it is easy to see that at least some of the behavioral strategies associated with the basic emotions are commonly turned on self as well as on others as we shift between emotions. For example, it is perfectly obvious that some people demandingly "boss" others while some people demandingly "boss" themselves, but for most "bosses," this kind of behavior is such an ingrained habit that it is regularly turned on both self and others. What is less obvious, but on reflection equally true, is that all of the behavioral strategies associated with the basic emotions are used in this way, so that we are always engaged in the very complex operation of trying to integrate, at any given moment, strategies that may be intended for self, for others, or for a continually and rapidly shifting and unpredictable combination of self and others.

3. The Fifth Emotion

🌿 Up to this point, we have said almost nothing about the fifth emotion, which we have conventionally labeled happiness; and in fact very little need be said about it. Why? Because it is a hypothesis of this book that the fifth emotion is what we naturally shift into when we are not being demanding, fearful, angry, or sad. We do not need to define it, locate it, seek it out. It is always there, waiting for us, as soon as we slow down our shifting.

Nor need the fifth emotion be an ineffable, ethereal, hard-to-reach state like the Buddhist Nirvana: it should be effortlessly, indeed automatically, available to anyone who is not gripped by unrelenting demands, anger, fear, or sadness. Moreover, with the possible exception of the most deeply disturbed, each of us should have experienced it, if only in flashes. We have all experienced moments when, in behavioral terms, we are ready to give up grabbing, avoiding, attacking, or giving up, when we are truly ready to "live and let live," and when we probably feel calm, secure, untroubled, and cheerful as well.

Is it really this simple? Yes and no. What is not so simple is learning how to stop shifting emotions at high speeds once one has become habituated to doing so. Subsequent chapters will be concerned with this question: how people stop shifting and come to enjoy themselves more. But for now, we will just try to clarify further what we are hypothesizing the fifth emotion is and is not.

Characteristics of the fifth emotion

What the fifth emotion is, in addition to a willingness to "live and let live" and feelings of calm, security, balance, and cheer, is a feeling of being connected, connected with other people, with a task, commonly with both, but in any case with something outside ourselves. We have already noted that emotions are highly reactive in nature, propelling us into some specific action or inaction, and also highly social, regulating our relations with other creatures and objects. When we are feeling unrestrained desire, fear, anger, or sadness, we are experiencing what has been referred to as "separating emotions," that is, we are feeling alienated from, rather than close to, others or the world around us. When we stop shifting rapidly and come to rest in the fifth emotion, we feel more connected to other people, to other creatures, to work undertaken in common with others, to nature, to the universe in general. Sometimes we feel so intensely connected that we can properly speak of loving other people, creatures, work in common, nature, the entire universe, but if so, it is a gentle, warm love, not a lustful, demanding, acquisitive love, which would exemplify unrestrained desire, nor a narrow connection with one group that just leads to an angry

---

* Connection leading to disconnection is discussed further in chapter six.

disconnection with another, allegedly opposing group, as when two countries go to war.*

Many religious traditions teach that what we are calling the fifth emotion, in essence a feeling of inclusiveness and connection, is in some sense true, while separating emotions such as unrelenting desires, fear, anger, or sadness are in some sense false. In Christianity, connectedness to one another and especially to God is a higher reality to be sought for, and failure to reach it brings a terrible price. In the Gospels, Jesus asks those about to be consigned to Hell: "Did you not know that the beggar, the homeless person you turned away was actually I?" In some forms of Hinduism and Buddhism, we are not only connected to each other and the universe, we are identical with one another, and both the feeling and the appearance of separation are illusions. But to state that connectedness somehow reflects a deeper or truer reality, or alternatively that we are not only connected but are in some sense identical with one another, or to say (as Karen Horney, Carl Rogers and other modern psychologists have said) that feelings we have described as calm, secure, balanced, cheerful, and connected reflect our "real" self while feelings we have described as agitated and disconnected reflect a "false" self—all these assertions take us into metaphysical regions beyond the scope of this book. For our purposes, it is enough to note that human beings are social, i.e., naturally connected creatures, and that the fifth emotion appears to be our normal, equilibrium position, the position that we naturally fall into when not shifting around the first four emotions.

When we are not shifting aimlessly, when we are not unrestrainedly desiring, afraid, angry, or sad, we just naturally feel calm, secure, balanced, cheerful and connected, along with a host of other, closely related feelings. These feelings, some of which are listed below, are all hypothesized to be aspects of or variations on the basic emotion of happiness, all elaborations and embellishments that our higher mental faculties invent as they experience and interpret what is still a

absorbed
accepting • active
affectionate • approving
aware • benign • comfortable
committed • compassionate • confident
contented • curious • empathetic • energetic
flexible • focused • forgiving • friendly • full of humor
generous • genuine • grateful • happy • imperturbable
interested • joyful • loving • modest • nonjudgmental
open • patient • peaceful • playful • realistic
refreshed • relaxed • respectful • serene
sincere • stimulated • supple
sympathetic • steady • tolerant
tranquil • unhurried
unselfconscious
warm

single, underlying, basic emotion, an emotion most readily summarized as happiness but which defies any single word description:

For most people, just reading these words makes us feel better, because these are "feel good" words. For that very reason, we are right to be skeptical. After all, what is actually meant here? Are any of these words measurable in any way? A state of emotional calm is usually recognizable from the outside and (in animal studies involving close human relatives such as baboons) has been crudely measured in terms of body chemistry. But is connectedness necessarily at the heart of it? And what about the other words listed? What about words such as "flexible," for example?

At this point, it is necessary to offer an important caveat concerning the use of words. With the exception of some technical or scientific terms, all words in English or any other language are handed down over time and become laden with emotional connotations. Hence if we think that a person is prone to change his or her thoughts or actions frequently, and we approve of this, we say that he or she is flexible. If we think that the person is prone to change thoughts or actions frequently but we do not approve, we do not say he or she is flexible; we say he or she is opportunistic, which has a less positive connotation. In this case, the trait being described could be similar if not identical to an objective observer; what changes is the way we have labeled it, either positively (it is good) in the case of flexible or negatively (it is bad) in the case of opportunistic. Whether a word such as "flexible" really means anything more than "I like it" has provoked much philosophical discussion. Suffice it to say for now that the combination of words we have associated with the fifth emotion, taken together, are intended to describe something more than "I like it" or "I do not like it." They are intended to describe a feeling of being part of something larger than oneself that helps one remain cheerful, calm, and rooted, a feeling that is deeply satisfying, and that can remain deeply satisfying for long periods of time.

Critiques of the fifth emotion

Even if the fifth emotion offers a calmer, more cheerful, and more connected way of life, is it correct to say that it is more satisfying, more enjoyable, more sustainable than the first four emotions? For example, a long-time inhabitant of the first emotion, desire, might argue that feelings of calm are for retirees, feelings of cheerfulness or connectedness are for children, that seeking to be calm, cheerful, and connected will interfere with what really matters in life, getting ahead, and that success in getting ahead will eventually bring all the calm, cheer, and connectedness one could want.

The initial notion, that the fifth emotion is somehow inactive or passive, is certainly wrong. People who are largely free of unrelenting desires, fear, anger, and sadness have much more energy to put into appealing projects and enterprises of all kinds. Nor is connectedness for children. A wise businessman observed that "everything we do in business or in life is about building relationships, everything." As we soon learn in life, the noise, commotion and panache of desiring and demanding rarely, if ever, help us build and maintain the durable relationships needed for success, much less help us develop genuine feelings of accomplishment and satisfaction.

Another first-emotion (desire) alibi, as it were, is that one can try to be calm, cheerful, and connected during ordinary times but not when life hurls its challenges and we must respond under stress. But, again, behavioral strategies rooted in intense desire just increase the stress and make handling challenges all the more difficult. For example, an athlete who enters a competition full of thoughts about himself or herself, about how he or she must win at all cost, about the humiliation of losing or making a mistake, is very unlikely to excel or win a medal. Only in learning how to hold onto the fifth emotion, even under the ultimate stress of world class competition, is it possible to perform at one's best. As an Olympic skating gold medalist observed: "It seems I had to quit caring too much to skate my best."[1] Similarly, a writer may think that he or she needs to "rev the engines" and demand more of him- or herself, but this will more likely lead to writer's block than to the great American novel, and angry attempts to boss, abuse, or whip oneself through the block will just make it worse.

Yet another first-emotion critique of the fifth emotion is that living there is somehow less intense, less absorbing, less alive, that one must at least eschew calm in order to explore life to the fullest. As Leonard Bernstein once said: "You can never have too much passion . . . "[2] There is at least a kernel of truth here. It is logically inescapable that people must experience all the emotions in order to experience all that life has to offer. And it is equally true that the first four emotions can be very interesting and absorbing, as we shall explore further in the next chapter, but that does not mean that the fifth emotion is not. A more reasonable evaluation is that each emotion can be equally absorbing, although the fifth emotion tends to be quietly and calmly absorbing, while the other emotions may go over the top with theatricality, melodrama, and desperation.

A peculiarly first-emotion position is to try to reject and embrace the fifth emotion at the same time. For example, an individual with unrestrained desires may concede that a calm, cheerful, and connected attitude makes us more popular or successful with others and then conclude that the answer is simply to fake such an attitude. In this vein, a twenty-seven-year-old wholesale meat dealer explained to a *Washington Post* reporter that appearing to have a sense of humor makes picking up girls easier: " . . . you've got to be able to make them laugh, if you don't you can't pick [them up]. You make 'em laugh, you got 'em. That's the bottom line."[3] Presumably this attitude well illustrates the difference between opportunism and flexibility, but it is routinely employed by salesmen of all sorts, including politicians. Presidents Johnson, Nixon, and Clinton were all reported to possess volcanic tempers, but none ever willingly displayed angry behavior in pub-

lic. One need only consider the difference between President Nixon's public statements and
the Watergate tapes that recorded his private
utterances, or the difference between President
Clinton's outwardly warm, nonconfrontational
style and the moment on the President's private
plane, Air Force One, recorded by the *Washington
Post's* Bob Woodward: "'Who the hell could make
such a dumb f*ck@#g mistake?' the president
bellowed . . . [and] . . . raged. . . . In the con-
fined spaces of the plane, Clinton stormed on and
on. It was truly awful, on the edge of controlled
violence. Clinton screamed. Gergen, watching
the outburst, was stunned. He had never quite
seen an adult, let alone a President, in such a
rage."[4]

So far we have mainly focused on how the fifth
emotion might be attacked, and in the process
misinterpreted, from a first-emotion position (that
is, a position of desire); but similar slings and
arrows might be shot from fearful, angry, or sad
redoubts as well. For example a businessman
inhabiting the third emotion, anger, might argue
that life is just constant warfare, a matter of
destroy or be destroyed, and that calm and connected states will just render one vulnerable, to
which an individual living in the fifth emotion
could reply that neither life nor business is about
warfare, but that even if it were, periods of rest
and building alliances with others would be
vitally necessary.

Similarly, a concert singer speaking from the
second emotion, fear, might say (as one actually
did): "My knees were knocking; my heart started

beating so hard, I thought it was going to come out of my chest; then it went down to my knees and I thought 'oh now, I won't be able to walk'— [but all this actually made me perform better]," to which a coach speaking from the fifth emotion might gently reply that a little less fear would have provided just as useful a stimulus. In either case, it might be reemphasized that people do not perform at their best while angry or fearful, unless being pursued by a wild predator. On the contrary, the best performers work through the anger or fear and use it as extra energy once they have gotten back to the fifth emotion. As former British Prime Minister Margaret Thatcher once explained the process: " How long have I been Prime Minister? About seven and one half years . . . [yet] every time I go in [to Parliamentary questioning] I [have] to think, 'Now look love, keep calm, concentrate.' If I go to Wimbledon or to the [soccer] Cup Final, I know exactly how those people feel when they walk out onto the pitch or onto the court—nervous, frightened to death until the game starts; they then lose themselves in the game [in effect becoming reconnected to something larger than themselves]."[5]

The fifth emotion as an equilibrium state

Is finding and sustaining the fifth emotion then the be-all and end-all of our lives, the goal for which we should all strive? Let us hope not. First of all, as noted above, one does not have to strive for the fifth emotion in order to find it. If we successfully detach ourselves from unrelenting desires and demands, fear, anger and sadness, we will more or less effortlessly shift into a place of calm, cheer, security, balance, and connected- ness. It does help, often, to keep that place in the corner of our eye. For example, before giving a speech it certainly helps to coach oneself through the fear as Margaret Thatcher habitually did. But it also helps to feel connected, if possible even to feel loving toward the group one is about to address, even if or especially if the group includes members of a competing party, because a sense of connectedness will help to pull one through and even transmute and put to use the raging emotions of desire, fear, anger or sadness to which one may otherwise fall prey.

At the same time, and importantly, finding the fifth emotion need not be regarded as the be-all or end-all of human life. The fifth emotion is simply emotional equilibrium, no more. As vital as emo- tional equilibrium is, it is only one aspect of physical and mental life, and if we glorify it or romanticize it or pursue it too zealously, we will simply find ourselves shifting back, however unwittingly, into what may be or become the torrid, maniacal depths of other, very different, emotions.

Part Two

EMOTIONS
AND VALUES

4. Conundrums of Choice

🔥 We have previously defined emotions in evolutionary and biological terms as those more primitive elements of our brain that are highly watchful, continually scanning the environment and modulating our energy level; highly social, regulating our relations with other creatures or objects; and highly reactive, often propelling us into one of five specific types of social action illustrated, at the most basic level, by taking (desire), avoiding (fear), attacking (anger), giving up or capitulating (sadness), and either, at a minimum, "living and letting live" or, better, connecting (happiness).

This short definition of emotion has proved serviceable, but we now need to expand it. First, we need to emphasize that emotion does more than just scan and regulate and react; it weighs choices and reaches conclusions, in particular weighs choices and reaches conclusions about personal values. Often this process is so instantaneous, so automatic that weighing and choosing pass virtually unnoticed. For example, most of us have a deep emotional commitment to staying alive, that is to say, we value staying alive highly, and if we run into a proverbial tiger, we flee in terror and do not pause to reflect on the underlying choice. But, under most circumstances, we have a much greater range of choice.

To explore this further, consider the still fairly primitive problem that we have previously cited of a schoolyard bully facing us down in the third grade (and assume that he represents a genuine threat and not just bluster). Under these circumstances, we will presumably not have a choice about whether to remain in the fifth emotion, but we will have some choice about whether to approach the problem from the fourth emotion by trying to placate the bully, perhaps by offering a candy bar; from the third emotion by angrily assaulting him, whatever the odds; from the second emotion by running away or at least practicing prudent avoidance; or from the first emotion by trying to get what we want (in this case for the bully to go away) by diverting him or talking our way out of it. To some degree, these choices will reflect our instantaneous assessment of what will succeed best. But our personal definition of success, and our willingness to try different strategies, will very much depend on our values, specifically our emotional values, even, in this case, the relatively fluid and untested emotional values that we have formed by the third grade.

Emotional values and choices

As previously stated, it is a hypothesis of this book that as we mature into adult human beings, most of us, most of the time, have the option of living in the fifth emotion, with only such forays into the first four emotions as are required to accommodate temporary challenges or crises. In other words, the fifth emotion is the normal, equilibrium state, and if we value it sufficiently, if we make the value judgment that we want to be there, and if we keep looking for it, we will eventually find that it is available. This observation notwithstanding, it appears that a great many adults, whether they realize it or not and whether they mean to or not, value the first four emotions very highly, often more highly than the fifth emotion, as evidenced by their long residence in the first four emotions, their reluctance to leave those emotions, or their tendency to want to combine emotions and emotion-related behavioral strategies that are inherently contradictory, such as wanting to be an angrily demanding boss (behavior associated with the third emotion) and also, simultaneously and confusedly, to be taken care of (behavior associated with the fourth emotion). Given this state of affairs, the question inevitably arises as to why people might end up valuing emotions or related behavioral strategies, or cling to emotions and strategies, or try to combine emotions and strategies that seem so inherently unrewarding, that often frustrate the stated goals of the individuals involved.

There are, of course, natural explanations, such as organic brain damage, but it would be surprising if most people turned out to be brain damaged.* There is also sleep deprivation, which quickly shifts us out of the fifth emotion and eventually plunges us into fearful and angry

---

* Recent research suggests that physical trauma to the brain in childhood might be more common and serious than previously supposed. In addition, emotional trauma may produce some organic brain damage, but the amount of damage hypothesized is not great, and the damage may be reversible. [1]

depths of paranoia, or demanding and sad depths of mania or despondency, but most of us are not chronically sleep-deprived. There is sun deprivation, which has been most closely linked to sadness, but which presumably affects all of our emotions. There are also variants on these ideas: perhaps we are not brain damaged but have nevertheless inherited a temperamental proclivity for anger; perhaps we are not sleep or sun deprived, but too much stress has "burned up" a vital brain chemical, and we are responding as if sleep or sun deprived. Conversely, perhaps our genes and brain chemicals are fine, but we have become conditioned to chronic anger or chronic depression or emotional instability by our life experiences, especially our childhood experiences, or have been taught to be angry or fearful or sadly passive by our family, our society, or our culture.

All of these explanations seem reasonable, although—as with all quasi-deterministic explanations—with the possible exception of organic brain damage or sleep or sun deprivation, they may be difficult to prove one way or the other (for example, it is impossible to prove or disprove that our genes make us chronically angry). In addition, they are all useful—paradoxically, as useful for people who do not want to change as for people who do. If you do not want to change, you can blame everything on your genes or society. If you do want to change, the first step may be shifting out of the despair of the fourth emotion, and to start the process it may be helpful to stop reproving yourself. For someone chronically depressed, who also hates being depressed, the last thing in the world that person needs to hear is: "stop moping, stop feeling sorry for yourself, stop being so selfish, it's all your own fault"—all the harsh criticisms, recriminations, and even insults that have been hurled by family members or friends and long since internalized.

Similarly, many therapists insist that alcoholics should see themselves as victims of a disease rather than as morally reprehensible abusers, even though there is not much more factual evidence for the disease model than for the immorality model, because the disease model helps and the immorality model does not or rarely does. And in a more or less analogous way, doctors may prescribe psychoactive medications—notwithstanding the toxicity and uncertain efficacy of these drugs, and our current lack of understanding of the physiology of emotions—mainly because they think it will help but also at least in part because the very use of a pill reassures the patient that he or she is not necessarily at fault, that it is a matter of biochemistry, even though, in actuality, if brain chemistry affects attitude and behavior, it seems likely that attitude and behavior would also affect brain chemistry. Even in less extreme cases, quasi-determinism has its uses. For example, a young woman comes to a therapist unhappy about always staying at home and never meeting anyone. After the patient is told that she was born an introvert and will always enjoy being alone, she becomes much more cheerful, and, ironically, more disposed to go out and meet people.

Whatever its uses, quasi-determinism offers less than a full story. All human actions may be presumed to contain elements of chemistry, conditioning, and choice, but the three are so interwoven that they cannot be completely disentangled by observation, logic, or any other reproducible means. Under these circumstances, it is choice that deserves our closest attention. As psychiatrist Viktor Frankl, a survivor of the Nazi death camps, has observed, no amount of heredity or conditioning can explain why one person in the camps behaved as a "swine" and another a "saint." Or as a successful Hispanic television actor has put it: "When I speak to kids who've ended up in jail, you know what I tell them? I tell them we're all given a choice. Some people say they didn't have a choice. They're poor or brown or crippled. They had one parent or no parents or foster parents. Well, you can [stop there]. . . . Or you can say, 'I'm not gonna let it stop me. I'm gonna make it be my strength.' And that's what I did. Because of where I was from and what happened to me, I had the choice of being either happy or sad. I chose to be happy."[2]

Why people choose as they do

So, we are left with at least some degree of choice, and with the question of why people, given some degree of choice, might actually choose to be demanding (unrestrained desire), fearful, angry, or even sad, although few people deliberately choose to be sad. And the answer, not surprisingly, is that most people are chronically demanding, fearful, angry, or even sad because, at heart, they either regard it as the right thing to do (more likely in the case of demanding or angry), or regard it as an unavoidable by-product of making other "right" choices. Like all human beings, they have had to develop emotional values, could not function without them, and these are the emotional values that they have developed, perhaps for good reasons, perhaps for good reasons that are no longer operable, perhaps for less good reasons.

Moreover, like all emotional values, patterns of being chronically demanding, afraid, angry, or sad provide a direction, an intensity, a meaning, even a deep meaning to life. Individuals who are chronically angry truly believe that other people have been unfair to them, that the world is a jungle, a place to eat or be eaten, and that they are engaged in a struggle to the death. The struggle is absorbing, interesting, challenging, hard to give up; to give it up would involve a great, almost an unendurable loss. Even if anger is not directly chosen, the related struggle, the related thought patterns, the related values are. As psychologists Robert Harper and Arthur Ellis argue in their *Guide to Rational Living*: "It is notable . . . that even highly negative feelings [represent] active participations in life; and that is perhaps why so many seemingly unhappy people resist giving up their severe feelings of depression or mania. Intense absorption seems to be the common denominator of practically all forms of aliveness—including even the emotionally disturbed forms."[3]

Of course, there are as many themes and variations as there are people. Some people who are temporarily or chronically demanding or angry regard their emotional value system, their emotional *Weltanschauung*, the emotional portion of their philosophy of life, as not only right, but good, moral, appropriate, fitting, and proper as well. Some others, in a depressed state, may find everything about their lives to be wrong and ill-fitting, perhaps even wrong and ill-fitting enough to inspire a decision to enter therapy, but still, perhaps infused with a certain tragic grandeur or at least a theatrical polish, intensely absorbing, and consequently very difficult to give up. As the female alter ego of a famous male Paris fashion designer explained this: "Deep down [the designer is] tortured and tormented. But he wouldn't change his situation for all the gold in the world. He's happy to be what he is, rather than some guy with a normal life. He's doing what he wants to do."[4]

It is easy to be dismissive of people who are holding on to values that (at least to outside observers) do not seem to be in their best interest. One writer, for example, in response to the question of why we sometimes do things we know (or at least suspect) are not good for us, has slyly suggested that "you gotta believe in something, and so maybe you believe you are the kind of person who, for example, deserves to stub your toe a lot. You wander around your house at night, barefoot, with the lights off, WHANG!, you're hopping up and down saying, 'I'm such an idiot!' Though blinded by pain, at least you know who you are."[5] But in the real world it is not so simple. As Viktor Frankl has correctly observed, "we must never leap to the conclusion that a neurotic's world-view is necessarily wrong simply because it is neurotic . . . .two times two equals four even if a paranoiac makes the statement. . . . It is equally false to judge the worth of a work of art by the fact that the artist created it in . . . a psychotic phase of his life. . . . Our evaluation of ideas [should] not depend on the psychic origin of those ideas."[6]

Fully conscious choices

Frankl's cautionary words are important because we are dealing with the realm of values, and in the realm of values no human being can expect to have all the answers, unless he or she thinks that he or she is God. Given our limitations, we can only repeatedly review the evidence, reaffirm what we have come to believe, and offer those beliefs as a free gift to anyone who wants them. Specifically, if we are going to try to help someone, either someone else or ourselves, deeply embedded in value systems related to the first four emotions, we must start by emphasizing that, although our emotional states do represent choices, the reason we have chosen the first four emotions is not because it makes us feel good, but rather because we have been taught, either by individuals or by circumstances, or have taught ourselves in bygone times, that this is the way we should feel. Furthermore, because most people have little or no idea that they have such choices—let alone how these choices are made—

they are as bound into their condition as if they had no choice at all; it is as if they were locked in a cell. It is not exactly a cell of their own making, as various New Agers might like to tell them; yet it's a cell whose door is not really locked. All that is required is to know that one can open the door and walk out.

In theory, because happiness (or equilibrium) is the default position, it should not be necessary to seek it. If we step out of the cell, it will be there, waiting for us. In practice, because we all need values in order to exist at all and are deathly afraid of losing the ones we have, it helps to identify the new values before giving up the old, and it especially helps if we can see that the new emotional values are at least as credible, intense, vibrant, absorbing, and meaningful as the old emotional values. Psychologist Stanton Peele tells the story of his Uncle Oscar, a labor organizer who could not stop chain smoking until a colleague pointed out that he had become a pawn of the American tobacco companies. This story is not ideal because it is really about the substitution of anger for desire, one dark emotion for another. By contrast, what we really need to do (if we are to stop over-using or abusing the emotion of unrestrained desire, that is if we are to abandon the philosophy of life that such over-use and abuse represents) is to make a fully conscious decision, a fully conscious value judgment that the fifth emotion and the underlying philosophy of life that it represents is the right emotion and the right philosophy for us.

How people typically go about or might go about the process of reconsidering their emotional values, in particular reconsidering whether the fifth emotion ought not to be valued more highly, will be covered in Part Three. In the meantime, in the remainder of Part Two, we will discuss further the relation between emotions and values, and also hypothesize how emotional values fit into the grander scheme of all our values. Those readers who may be more interested in the "how to" of our emotions than in trying to illuminate the relationship of emotions and values may to go directly to Part Three.

5. A Further Word on Emotional Values

In the preceding chapter, we introduced the idea that emotions are not just the more primitive elements of our brain that continually scan the environment, regulate our relations with other creatures or objects, and often propel us into some specific social action such as taking (desire), avoiding (fear), attacking (anger), capitulating (sadness), and either "living and letting live" or positively connecting (happiness). In addition, although initially it may sound odd, emotion represents a way of weighing choices and reaching conclusions, in particular a way of choosing personal values and then making further choices based on those values. So it is that when we blow up at our boss and tell him or her to go fly a kite rather than counting to ten to let the anger pass, we are certainly making a choice and expressing a personal value judgment.

Given this complex interplay between emotion and values, is it more accurate to think of emotions giving rise to values, values giving rise to emotions, or are both emotions and values simply different sides of the same coin? Actually, all three views are equally defensible, as the following schematic summary suggests:

- I rely on my mind to interpret the world.
- In part, I rely on the emotional portion of my mind.
- When I rely on the emotional portion of my mind, I will be living in desire, fear, anger, sadness, or happiness, or I may be rapidly shifting through all of them.
- As I grow up, I develop decided preferences for one basic emotion or another. Implicitly I rank the emotions.
- These rankings represent my primary emotional value judgment. In effect, I emphasize desire or anger or happiness or de-emphasize them as the case may be.*
- Although an emphasis on desire may represent my primary emotional value judgment, living with an emphasis on desire also leads me to other value judgments (secondary emotional value judgments).
- Because emotions are highly social, regulating my relations with other creatures, secondary value judgments usually concern groups of people, groups of people we value or do not value.
- Groups of people we value or do not value emotionally may be defined on a concrete, everyday level (as in family or work group),

---

* Although most people would probably claim to emphasize happiness, many do not actually do so for reasons already outlined in Chapter Five.

on a somewhat more abstract level (as in neighborhood or nation), or on a very abstract level (as in class, race, all of humanity, or history, that is, humanity projected into past and future).

- Groups of people so defined (families, nations, races) may be thought of as tribes, whether tribes we profess to value or tribes we profess not to value. Very often the tribes we value or do not value are defined in terms of each other (hence a youth gang member feels justified in shooting anyone living on Irvine Street but must come to the assistance of anyone living on Jones Street—in effect, one cannot be defined except in terms of the other).

- Secondary emotional values can thus be thought of primarily as tribal values.

- Although emotions regulate our social relations, that is, our relations with other creatures, human beings tend to confuse creatures and objects on an emotional level. In some cases, we treat other creatures as objects; in other cases, we treat objects as creatures. Even when we keep the two apart perceptually, the two realms still overlap. We may have a very strong desire for a fancy house or car, but this may primarily reflect a desire to improve our tribal status (our standing within our family, our city, our profession, our country, etc.). Thus, our secondary emotional values may come to focus on tribally related objects as well as on tribes *per se*.

Up to this point, we have described emotion as a mental process whose product is an instantaneous emotional reaction or value judgment.* The emotional value judgment may either be primary (relating to the basic emotion preferred) or secondary (relating to the tribe or object selected on the basis of the preferred basic emotion). Regardless of whether the value judgment is primary or secondary, it will typically consist of both an underlying belief and an evaluation, as diagrammed on the following pages.

---

* The term "value judgment" itself may have an unfortunate negative emotional connotation for some, implying a harsh or critical stance. But the phrase in this context is not meant to connote harshness, negativism, or any other angry emotion.

PRIMARY EMOTIONAL VALUE JUDGMENTS

Primary Emotional Value Judgment	Expressed as a Belief	Expressed as an Evaluation
Desire	"I believe that everything should, ought, must be a certain way, that I cannot live with it any other way, and that I have every right to boss myself and others to get it the way I want it."	"Life is great (I am getting my way) or terrible (I am not)."
Fear	"I believe that I will die if I enter this airplane [or similar] and/or I will 'die' from wounded pride if people think badly of me [or if I think badly of myself]"	"Airplanes/ people are frightening."
Anger	"I believe that people and the world are unfair to me, and I have every right to scorn, blame, and abuse."	"The world or other people deserve to be punished."
Sadness	"I believe I have lost some-thing forever and/or have made unforgiveable mistakes."	"Life is hope-less."
Happiness	"I believe that feeling calm, cheerful, and connected are more important than always getting what I want (some-times I will, sometimes I will not), more important than protecting my own pride or worrying what others think, more important than defend-ing my own views of fairness and unfairness, and more important than dwelling on past losses or mistakes. I believe that the world is a place where, most of the time, I can feel calm, cheerful, and connected."	"Most of the time, I appre-ciate and enjoy life."

SECONDARY EMOTIONAL VALUE JUDGMENTS

(Imagine a typical tribal scene, perhaps a teenage high school class, in which one member of the class finds another attractive.)

Primary Emotional Value Judgment	Secondary Emotional Value Judgment Expressed as a Belief	Secondary Emotional Value Judgment Expressed as an Evaluation
Desire	"I believe he/she is attractive."	"I want him/her."
Fear	"I believe that my pride will be shattered if he/she rejects me."	"He/she is frightening."
Anger	"I believe his/her refusal to see me is completely unfair."	"He/she deserves whatever he/she gets."
Sadness	"I believe he/she is much better than I am."	"It's hopeless to think he/she would ever look at me."
Happiness	"I believe he/she is not only attractive, but a nice person."	"I would enjoy being close to him/her."

6. Emotions, Values, and Actions

❦ If the sample emotional value judgments laid out in the last chapter seem simple, even primitive, it is because emotional responses are simple, no matter how elaborated they may become as they ricochet around our mind and are interpreted and reshaped by the higher cognitive faculties. Above all, these emotional value judgments are energetically action-oriented, since emotion is meant both to direct action and to supply or to drain energy. In actuality, of course, everything is so closely and instantaneously interrelated that the action is often implicit in the preceding evaluation (the phrase "He deserves a good, swift kick" both evaluates and defines a desired action). In some cases, the action may even precede the emotion (note, for example, William James's famous observation that a deliberate refusal to cry may help forestall sadness, or the discovery of emotionally turbulent people that if they stabilize their outside with a regular job or family responsibilities, they may help stabilize their inside as well).

In any case, by adding an action column, we may now obtain a more complete picture of how emotions give rise to value judgments, which in turn may be expressed either as beliefs or evaluations, which in turn give rise to concrete, energetic, and sometimes dramatic actions (which in turn lead to further emotions):

Primary Emotional Value Judgment	Secondary Emotional Value Judgment Expressed as a Belief	Secondary Emotional Value Judgment Expressed as an Evaluation	Possible Corresponding Action*
Desire	"I believe she is beautiful and that she'll find me very attractive as well."	"I want her, she's beautiful, she's mine."	Aggressively demand a date.
Fear	"I believe she will reject me."	"She is terrifying."	Flee her presence or at least avoid it.
Anger	"I believe she has been unfair to me."	"I have every reason to hate her."	Attack (verbally or physically).
Sadness	"I believe I am a loser who always gets it wrong."	"It's hopeless to think she would ever look at me."	Do nothing, or grovel at her feet.
Happiness	"I believe she is a wonderful person."	"I would enjoy being close to her."	Ask her out.

* By no means the only possible corresponding action. Other less extreme versions of these actions may result, or the nonemotional brain may hold the emotions in check and redirect or arrest action, as we shall discuss in the next chapter.

Although two people can form a tribe, most of our tribal associations and decisions involve larger numbers. To choose a lurid example, consider, on the following page, the case of someone living in Germany, after Hitler has seized power, who is considering whether to join the Nazi party.

Primary Emotional Value Judgment	Secondary Emotional Value Judgment Expressed as a Belief	Secondary Emotional Value Judgment Expressed as an Evaluation	Possible Corresponding Action
Desire	"I believe the party offers the surest route to advancement."	"I will become more successful and powerful by joining."	Join the party.
Fear	"I believe it will be safest to join the party."	"I am afraid not to join the party."	Join the party.
Anger	"I believe the Nazis are right to hate Jews, Communists, and foreigners."	"Jews, Communists, and foreigners are hateful."	Attack Jews, Communists, and foreigners by joining the party.
Sadness	"I believe Hitler is the kind of supreme leader I can follow unthinkingly."	"I need a supreme leader I can follow unthinkingly."	Surrender one's own independent judgment and will by joining the party.
Happiness	"I believe the Nazi party exemplifies the worst and most primitive traits of the first four emotions."	"The Nazi party is barbaric."	Do not join the party.

The important point to take from all of this is that emotions, emotional values, and actions are so closely linked that they are virtually synonymous; that with emotions as with everything else in life there are choices to be made; and that if one spends most of one's life in anger, this is not solely because one's life situation dumped you there. What to do with one's life or whom to live with are value choices, but so are such fundamental questions as whether to be angry most of the time. Presumably Hitler, Stalin, Jesus, Einstein, and the Buddha were all sufficiently human to be tossed into all five basic emotions. But, in the end, each chose to value certain emotions more highly than others, to value them in very different ways, and each of us confronts the same choice in our lives.

It should be acknowledged, once again, that the numbering and description of the emotions presented here is merely a hypothesis, one that will eventually have to be tested by more advanced techniques of brain chemistry than we presently have. Moreover, other investigators have had, and continue to have, different views both about the number of emotions and about their role. For example David Viscott, in *The Language of Feelings*[1], suggests that one's emotions should be liberated from value judgments, that not only are the two separate and distinct, but that, in some important sense, they are actually antithetical to one another. The Harvard philosopher Robert Nozick agrees with this author that emotions involve an evaluation as well as a belief, but holds that emotions and values are separate phenomena, that emotions merely "inform us of the evaluations we are making" or "provide an analog model of the [underlying] value,"[2] although if true, this distinction may not be too important, because Nozick would presumably agree that emotions involve value judgments and choices.[3]

The idea that emotions represent a mental process designed to produce emotional values, and thus actions, has an especially radical implication for the centuries-old quest to define basic human emotional "needs" (as opposed to mere "wants"), a quest that has intrigued many philosophers and psychologists. For example, Sigmund Freud (1922) referred to two basic emotional needs (aggression and sex), Abraham Maslow (1954) referred to five (safety, security, love, self-esteem, self-actualization), and David C. McClelland and J. W. Atkinson (1958) referred to, and tried to measure, three (achievement, affiliation, and power). The general idea here is that whereas the body requires food, water, clothing, and shelter, the emotions by analogy must also have some basic needs which, if not satisfied, will lead to dysfunction. But, once one begins to see emotion as a way of weighing choices and reaching conclusions, in particular a way of weighing choices and reaching conclusions about personal values, it should be apparent that our only real emotional "need" is to have something to value, to be able to choose an emotion, an emotion-derived behavioral strategy, and a related series of actions, something that all of us will do in any case, although some of us will be more satisfied with our choices than others.

Leaving genuine mental illness aside, in which the entire brain, not just the emotional part, malfunctions from some organic cause, this book hypothesizes that emotional difficulties do not arise because of a lack of security or achievement or self-esteem or some other hard to define abstraction. On the contrary, people need food, water, clothing, shelter, and strong, workable emotional values that put them in the right emotions at the right time; if they have these, they can probably survive the absence of almost anything else.

7. The Wheel of the Mind

When we first introduced the idea of five basic emotions, we discussed each one—desire, fear, anger, sadness, and happiness—in isolation. We did this because it simplified the discussion, even though in actuality, as we soon saw, all the emotions continually interacted with, shaped and redefined each other, as schematically rendered in chapter one:

FIFTH EMOTION:

- Emotional states related to **happiness**, expressed as calm, cheer, balance, enjoyment, appreciation
- In behavioral terms, predisposed to "live and let live," or, better, to connect with people, activities, or objects

FOURTH EMOTION:

- Emotional states related to **sadness**
- In behavioral terms, predisposed to giving up, passivity, dependence, or submission; greatest good: being assisted or taken care of; greatest risk: masochism

FIRST EMOTION:

- Emotional states related to **desire**
- In behavioral terms, predisposed to taking, seizing, grabbing, demanding, bossing; greatest good: possessing X, Y, or Z; greatest risk: addiction

THIRD EMOTION:

- Emotional states related to **anger**
- In behavioral terms, predisposed to fighting, attacking, scorning, blaming; greatest good: dominance, revenge; greatest risk: sadism

SECOND EMOTION:

- Emotional states related to **fear**
- In behavioral terms, predisposed to avoidance, flight, nervousness; greatest good: independence; greatest risk: isolation

Now the time has come to expand the discussion still further by acknowledging that emotions represent only one kind of mental activity, and therefore only one source of personal values, albeit for many people the most compelling mode of mental activity and the deepest source of personal values. Moreover, the primary modes of internal mental activity—described here as emotion, logic, sense experience, and intuition—not only represent different ways of weighing choices, reaching conclusions, and forming values. They also continually interact with and shape

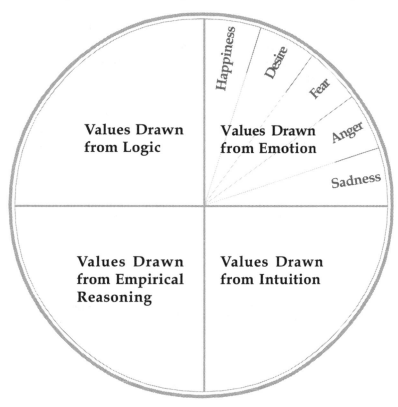

and redefine each other, so that all our value choices inevitably reflect more than one way of interpreting the world. In effect, emotional values, important as they are, reside in a larger framework encompassing emotional, logical, empirical, and intuitive values, as schematically rendered on the preceding page.

The definition of specific mental modes,* the ways they interact, the multiple perspectives from which each of us forms and expresses our values, will be left for Part Three. For the moment, the key point to emphasize is that any of the four mental modes—logic, sense experience, intuition, or emotion, that is, any of the modes through which we form our values—may itself malfunction. One type of malfunction is for one mode to become so dominant that other modes become completely subordinated. To take an extreme example, a person with a severe head injury may become uncontrollably emotional. Another type of malfunction is

---

* With respect to "mental modes," it should perhaps be noted that when we refer to logic or empirical reasoning, it is customary to use the term "thinking," as in logical or empirical thinking, or the term "cognition" (logic and empiricism representing different forms of cognition). Whether the terms "thinking" and "cognition" should be applied to intuition or especially to emotion is hotly debated. Since I believe this is mostly a semantic debate about appropriate terminology, without a scientifically right or wrong answer, I have tried to avoid the debate entirely by not using the term "thinking" or "cognition" but rather referring to intuition and emotion as mental activity modes or simply mental modes.

It should also be emphasized that the four mental modes do not correspond to the Jungian terms "thinking, feeling, sense perception, intuition"[1] which are utilized in the popular Briggs-Myers personality test. For example, Jung says that feelings in his lexicon are not emotions and instead refer to all value judgments (i.e., the three other categories do not involve value judgments).

internal to a mode. The empirical mind ceases to be reliably factual, the logical mind ceases to be truly logical, the emotional mind, whose job is to connect even more than disconnect, just disconnects us, especially from other people. The two types of malfunctions are of course related. One may become too dependent on mode X because mode Y is failing. Thus "cognitive" psychologists believe that emotions become too dominant when logical and empirical powers become too attenuated. A less restrictive view is to see all three modes potentially enhancing each other rather than holding one another in check.

In any case, expanding our horizons beyond emotions in this way reminds us that the human mind is highly dynamic, so that, just as the five basic emotions affect each other, so do the four mental modes. It also reminds us that emotional disturbance is usually better characterized as mental disturbance, since all four mental modes will inevitably become involved; that either emotional or broader mental disturbance (apart from that caused by organic brain damage) is not just a disturbance in our ability to interpret the world, but also in our ability to sort and choose values; that resolving disturbances will almost always require us to change our values at least to some degree; and, finally and rather hopefully, that there is always more than one way to go about changing our values, so that if one path does not lead anywhere, there is usually another path to try, as we shall see in Part Three.

Part Three

EMOTIONS, VALUES, AND THERAPIES

8. Indirect Emotional Therapies

❦ Acknowledging that many of one's values have become obsolete, distasteful, or even self-destructive is one thing. Doing anything about this acknowledgment is quite another. Precisely because human beings depend so completely on their values (as just noted, all anyone really needs to live are provisions, shelter, and values), it seems that earlier choices quickly become set, if not in concrete, at least in glue.

Sometimes it is effective to confront the old patterns directly. For example, in Chapter Four we referred to Stanton Peele's story of his Uncle Oscar, the labor organizer, who overcame a lifelong smoking habit by thinking of cigarette companies as greedy and malevolent. In this case, one gripping emotion, to smoke, is knocked out by an even more gripping emotion, to defy corporate America, or in the language of this book, an emotional valuation based on desire is overcome or at least redirected by shifting to a different valuation based on anger. In a variant of this idea, Uncle Oscar might have pledged that if he failed to stop smoking by a certain date, he would send a financial contribution to the politician whose policies or persona he most loathed.

So long as the substituted emotion of anger is neither disproportionally violent nor persists too long after it serves its purpose of getting rid of the cigarettes, this may not be such a bad tactic, but it is not always best to "fight fire with fire," and in any case does not bring Uncle Oscar closer to the fifth emotion. Perhaps a better alternative would be for Oscar to decide that he loved his family too much to leave them in the lurch by an untimely death, and thus to use the positive feelings of the fifth emotion directly to loosen the grip of the first emotion.

Contrariwise, depending on the individual and circumstances, it might be better still to change our emotional values indirectly by shifting as gently as possible out of emotion into an entirely different mental mode, another mode where our minds may be a little less turbulent and where we may cling less fixedly to the old. Whatever the particular emotional problem, whether an inability to give up smoking or a more general tendency to be angry all the time, if our emotional minds and value judgments are distorted, our logical, empirical, and intuitive mind and value judgments will be distorted as well. Indeed the most serious forms of mental disturbance involve delusions about fact (emotional and empirical malfunction) and paranoia (emotional and logical malfunction). But depending on circumstances and on the person, the distortions are probably less severe in one mental mode than another, and if one sincerely wants to review or change one's values, it should be easier to start with the less troubled mode.

This interconnection and interdependence of both mental modes and basic emotions explains why there is such a proliferation of therapies for emotional disturbance and why these therapies seem to work for some and not for others, and even then irregularly. In effect, without conceptualizing the situation in this way, some therapists are approaching through one mental mode or basic emotion, and others are approaching through another, in a rather ill-defined and hit-or-miss fashion that may or may not fit the mental preferences and habits of the patient. But this observation puts us a bit ahead of our story. For the moment, we need to concentrate on the proposition that it is possible to change emotional value judgments both directly, by emotional means, and indirectly, by trying to shift as far as possible out of the emotions into the logical, empirical, or intuitive portion of our mind. In this section, we will first review a large number of therapies organized in this way, beginning with the indirect approaches first, continuing on to the direct approaches, and then conclude both with an overview of therapies and an attempt to integrate them, with a word along the way about a particular "integrative" therapy that best reflects the "logic" and outlook of this book.

Indirect approach one: Changing emotions through logic

At first glance, this idea may seem a bit ludicrous. How can one change a deeply rooted emotion with something as abstract and seemingly superficial as logic? But logic is not superficial. It too is deeply rooted in the human psyche; it too has an almost atavistic hold on us. Even small children exhibit logical thinking and become emotionally agitated if logic is defied, especially if the illogic is connected to an apparent injustice: "You gave him a candy bar, you have to give me one too." It is true that children only respond to the most basic forms of logic, as in the example above. If a very small child is afraid of the dark, one does not point out that this fear is illogical. Instead one typically puts on a bathroom light, so the child can literally see (empirically confirm) that there is nothing there, or one finds a way to inject humor into the situation without making fun of the child (an intuitive technique), or one just gives the child a hug (a direct emotional technique).

In general, logic demands of us that we think 1) in an orderly way, beginning at an appropriate place and proceeding to a conclusion, 2) in an organized way, with different objects distinguished and differentiated, 3) in a consistent way, not overtly contradicting ourselves, 4) in a relevant way, not straying off the subject, 5) in a complete way, not leaving out important facts, and 6) as clearly as possible, not intentionally or unintentionally obfuscating. No matter what our age, we become extremely uneasy if we recognize, or if it is pointed out to us, that we are violating these rules. No matter how often violated, they are part of our core equipment and core tenets as human beings.

For example, at the start of the brief war between the United States and Iraq after Saddam Hussein's invasion of Kuwait in 1991, a television newscaster reported that "The Iraqis are putting out war propaganda, but the U.S. military is also intentionally putting out unreliable or even deceptive news. You have to listen and decide which accounts seem consistent with one another. If they are consistent, then you can believe them."[1] And we collectively nod our heads in agreement because we believe deeply in consistency as a guide to the truth, as per test #3 above. On the other hand, we often completely fail to discern when we are being illogical, as when one spouse tells another spouse to stop being bossy, but misses the fact that this directive is itself bossy and thus self-contradictory (the first spouse should instead say to the second: "be as bossy as you like, but I'll still do as I wish").

During the latter half of this century, a number of therapists have relied upon our innate reverence for logic, together with our usual lack of training in it, to help patients with even the most severe emotional problems. For example, Milton H. Erickson (1901-1980) illustrated a technique he called "utilization" (starting with the patient's own beliefs and drawing logical inferences) by asking a schizophrenic man who thought he was Jesus Christ, and who refused to participate in any of his hospital's mental health programs, if he were a carpenter. When the man agreed that, being Jesus, he indisputably was a carpenter, Erickson asked for and obtained his help in the hospital wood shop. In another instance, a woman told Erickson that she planned to commit suicide in six months. He responded that since she had a relatively short time to live, she would have to get busy and get a number of things done, starting with a trip to the hair salon. When she objected that this would be too expensive, he rejoined that with so little time left to live there was no point in saving money.[2] In each case, patients with a deep emotional disturbance did not want to be caught in a logical error, indeed the emotional disturbance made them all the more rigidly logical, and this was used to help them start to make changes in their emotional values and thus in their lives.

Indirect approach two: Changing emotions through sense experience (empirical reasoning)

Just as we are genetically endowed with emotion and logic, so we are also endowed with empirical powers, that is, with the capacity to gather in a wide variety of evidence through our eyes, ears, skin, tongue, and nose and to draw conclusions directly from that evidence. As Sergeant Friday said on the 1950s television show *Dragnet* about police work in California, "We just want the facts, Ma'am, just the facts." An individual oriented in this way will naturally de-emphasize emotion, but may find logic distasteful as well. In the first place, viewed through an empiricist's lens, logic may seem too abstract, too prone to generalize and simplify what should not be generalized or simplified, too far removed from the concrete, specific, often vivid, often intensely personal evidence of our own senses. Moreover, logic depends heavily on initial premises, and false premises can lead us down a perfectly reasoned road to perdition. In this sense, even Hitler or Stalin may be said to have been logical, given their warped initial premises.

Arguments against "emotional therapies" based on logic and in favor of therapies based on sense experience are probably as old as humanity, certainly at least several thousand years old. For example, the ancient Roman philosopher and statesman Seneca, tutor of the infamous Emperor Nero, agreed that "unbridled emotions"[3] are a curse, that emotional "equanimity"[4] is a blessing, that equanimity depends almost entirely "on one's thinking,"[5] but then dismissed logical approaches to achieving equanimity as empty and often misleading word games: "Mouse is a syllable, and a mouse nibbles cheese; therefore a syllable nibbles cheese."[6] In an aside that could just as easily have been written in our own era, he lambasted philosophers employing logical techniques for having "descended to the level of drawing distinctions between the uses of different syllables and discussing the proper meanings of prepositions and conjunctions. They have come to envy the philologist and the mathematician . . . with the result that they know more about devoting care and attention to their speech . . . than to their lives."[7]

Seneca even gently reproved the founder of his own Stoic philosophy, Zeno, for trying to prove that overdrinking is bad through a logical syllogism rather than by relying on "facts" and "examples," by far the best teachers.[8] In this view, people mentally stray from "facts and examples" at their peril, and if they would only pay closer attention to them, they would soon see that "craving . . . health, pleasure, good looks, political advancement and . . . other . . . enticing prospects" or, alternatively, "fearing exertion, death, pain, disgrace and limited means"[9] just brings us endless and needless emotional suffering. The philosophy of sense experience as expressed by Seneca even helps us come to grips with the inevitable end of experience in death, by reminding us that "it's rather rash to condemn a thing one knows nothing about," especially when one does know that for "many people it's a blessing."[10]*

Seneca's central supposition—that we should train ourselves to look at, hear, touch, smell, and taste the world around us, not passively but actively, in order to learn as much as possible, and that this knowledge will help us maintain good emotional health—is now supported by a number of more formal empirical studies. For example, when students have been strapped to a couch in a blackened, noiseless room, and thus deprived of most sense contact with the outside world, they begin to hallucinate and experience bizarre, quasi-psychotic thoughts within several days. For obvious reasons, these experiments have not been extended

---

* Ironically, the first part of Seneca's statement is a logical as well as empirical argument because there is an implied appeal to consistency. In effect an assertion is being made that it would be inconsistent to rely primarily on sense experience for one's judgments and then to condemn the state of being dead, about which we can never have any empirical knowledge. The second part of Seneca's statement is purely empirical because we can see with our own eyes how miserable people can be prior to death.

further, since they might lead to a complete or even irreversible emotional breakdown.[11]

On a more positive note, a variety of experiments have demonstrated that human beings find it emotionally calming and restorative to look at nature, even if only slides of forests or mountains, a few fish swimming in a fish tank, or a hospital window looking out at a lawn or tree.[12] Similarly, someone about to step on stage to deliver a speech can usually calm his or her emotions by looking very intently at the surrounding space—focusing on every architectural detail of the walls, ceiling, or decoration. To some degree, this works because it pulls the speaker out of the future (worry about the speech) or the past (thinking about speeches that went poorly) into the more concrete, immediate, and usually less threatening present. To some degree it works by distracting the speaker from his or her anxieties, and distraction is one of the most reliable empirical techniques. We all know people who, if you try to discuss an emotional problem, or especially if you try to analyze it in a logical way, just get more and more upset. Such people usually respond better to changing the subject, a distraction technique, which allows them to regain emotional equilibrium in their own way. Some particularly troubled individuals carry distraction to an extreme by continually traveling, changing jobs, or changing spouses, but the urge to explore the surrounding world in all its rich variety and detail, even completely lose oneself in the exploration, normally benefits rather than detracts from emotional health.

Although distraction is a tried and true empirical technique, modern empirically based therapists rely more heavily on its seeming opposite—immersion. If you are anxious about making speeches, try to make as many as possible. If you are afraid of flying, try to force yourself onto an airplane and keep doing it—usually at least twenty-one times—until taking a plane becomes as habitual as avoiding planes used to be. Although Seneca would applaud the spirit of so-called behaviorist exercises, which directly rely on sense experience to overcome emotional problems, he would also warn us against the money-changing merchants in the behaviorist temple who want to sell us on therapeutic quick fixes for every little inconvenience that we confront in life. As he noted about the ancient Roman world, "once you let [this] sort of person . . . into your house . . . you'll have someone regulating the way you walk and watching the way you use your jaws as you eat, and in fact going just as far as your patience and credulity [permit]."[13]

It has been argued that empirically based therapies or approaches to life—even the indisputably useful ones—are a bit superficial, that they mechanistically skim the surface and try to make us a bit more comfortable, only in the end to trivialize us. But this is very far from a complete view. The votaries of refined and accumulated sense experience have a great deal of wisdom, not just clever life strategies, to teach. For example, only empiricism can show us—not only tell us, but demonstrate to us—that contrary to our expectations, everything that happens to us will prove to be ambiguous, to involve some mixture of seemingly desirable and seemingly undesirable outcomes. No outcome in and of itself can be said to be purely good or purely bad, what seems good may lead to something bad and vice versa. If I am John Kennedy, I win the presidency of the United States, which seems good, only to be assassinated a few years later. Conversely, if I lose a job, which seems bad, I may unexpectedly get a much better job, and no one can ever predict exactly what will happen. As the Dalai Lama has said: "Bad things happen. For example, although we lost [Tibet], we get to meet many people [around the world] we otherwise would never have seen."[14]

But, on a deeper level, how should an empiricist react to the pell-mell, unpredictable, often unpleasant nature of sense experience? According to Joseph Alsop, a powerful Washington journalist after World War Two, later a political and art historian, and always an empiricist *par excellence* in his own approach to living, one should never hope for an easy life. " . . . The older I become and the more I see of the . . . world in which we live, the more I cherish my memories of being unceremoniously packed off to [boarding school at a young age], of being hurled into jobs without preparation, of going off to war and being, in stages, [shot at], imprisoned and then released. For me, these were liberating episodes in the sense that I found out about myself and, with each new discovery, could cross off the list one more damn thing it was foolish to be afraid of."[15] And writing about Franklin Roosevelt's fight with polio, he adds: "In the lives of the more fortunate modern Americans . . . , no value at all is now placed on [sense] experience, except for obviously pleasurable experience. Danger is regarded with horror, pain with loathing, even mere disappointment with pouting alarm. . . . But I would remind you that all reasonably strong [persons] always gain by experience and not least by really hard experience."[16]

The very nature of looking, listening, learning is that each individual will look, listen, and learn a bit differently. There may be only one logical correct answer, but there is never just one lesson to be learned from sense experience. Consequently, Alsop's tough-mindedness is not necessarily the only, or even the most likely, conclusion to be reached. Psychologist Carl Rogers agreed with Alsop that [sense] experience is our great teacher and that "a person is a fluid process, not a fixed and static entity, a flowing river of change, not a block of solid material, a continually changing constellation of potentialities, not a fixed quantity of traits."[17] But he himself learned to be soft, open, relaxed, receptive to its lessons, rather than tough and strong and immune to its slings and arrows. Nor was he much concerned with the "product" or outcome, the sense that suffering, like Roosevelt's, is toward a purpose, but rather celebrated the "process," the knowledge that we are forever in a state of becoming, and that we can never know in advance exactly where the adventure will take us or how it will end.

Indirect approach three: Changing emotions through a combination of logic and sense experience

As we have seen in the prior two sections, logic and sense experience represent different kinds of mental activity (mental modes), and the inherent differences can easily lead to conflict. On the other hand, logic and sense experience need not always be in conflict. In some instances they can be used together in a complementary or mutually supportive way, and if so, the psychical power of each can be greatly amplified. As previously noted, even a mental patient may be greatly impressed by logic, and an appeal to both fact and logic can be even harder to disregard.

The philosopher William James was quite correct in arguing that complete "originality cannot be expected in a field like [psychology] where all the attitudes and tempers that are possible have been exhibited in literature long ago."[18] So it should not be surprising that the idea of combining logic and sense experience to nudge us toward difficult emotional changes, like the idea of using logic or sense experience alone, can at least be inferred from the writings of ancient philosophers, including Epicurus in Greece and Epictetus in Rome and Greece and the Buddha in India, although thereafter little was heard about it until the twentieth century. Alfred Adler, Freud's colleague and then opponent, may perhaps be credited with reintroducing a therapy based on the notion that thinking directly shapes emotions and behavior, which echoed Epictetus' dictum that "Man is not disturbed about things but by his opinion about things" and the Buddha's similar assertion that "Everything is mind-made."[19] Many philosophers, including David Hume, William James, Alfred Ayer,[20] Bertrand Russell, John Dewey, and Alfred Korzybski [21] have also either echoed this idea or discussed the interplay of logic, empiricism, and emotion, but from a philosophical or linguistic perspective, usually not from a therapeutic perspective.

In the 1940s and 1950s Karen Horney radically altered classical Freudian analysis by bringing empirical observation front and center, by really watching and listening to her patients in a way that Freud claimed to do but rarely did, and then by encapsulating her brilliant empirical observations in a logical model of human behavior, albeit a logical model considerably weaker than the observations underlying it. Finally, in the 1950s Albert Ellis, and then Aaron Beck, deliberately combined logic and empiricism into "rational-emotive" and "cognitive" therapy respectively, which together—under the overall rubric of "cognitive therapy"—have increasingly come to dominate the emotional therapeutic field.

In Albert Ellis' particular formulation of a logico-empirical therapy, "human beings differ enormously in what brings them positive contentment, [but] they are remarkably alike in what makes them [emotionally] miserable."[22] ". . . Emotional pain or disturbance . . . usually originates in some [unfactual] or illogical ideas. The job of the neurotic is to uncover . . . [these] ideas; to see clearly the misinformation and illogic behind these ideas; and . . . change [them]. . . ."[23] It would be going too far, Ellis notes, to suppose that all emotional unhappiness stems from misinformation or illogic. He quotes approvingly Bertrand Russell's observation that "Any man who maintains that happiness comes wholly from within should be compelled to spend thirty-six hours in a blizzard, without food."[24] But most people who come for therapy are neither blizzarded nor starving; they have simply become habituated to thinking unfactually or illogically. Moreover, of the two, unfactual thinking can be worse: "Although . . . illogical thinking frequently leads to some degree of emotional disturbance, . . . magical [deeply unfactual] thinking tends to bring about even more pernicious results."[25]

In Ellis' view, it does not help a person with distorted thinking to uncover, "analyze," or "understand" in the classical psychoanalytic way. There may not be any apparent roots. Even if there are, even if an angry patient has been abused by parents, it may just make him or her angrier to perceive this. Nor does it help to ventilate the troubling emotions: this will also just tend to make them stronger. The only real relief comes from staying in the present and uncovering and challenging the patient's distorted thoughts as of this moment in time. Moreover, virtually all distorted thinking—unfactual and illogical—can be reduced to three basic beliefs:

- I must always be competent and successful and earn the approval of others.

- People must treat me fairly or they are "rotten."

- I must get my way at all times or I will be miserable.

These three beliefs are indeed both unfactual (there is no empirical evidence to support them) and illogical (refer back to the six tests listed at the beginning of the section on logical therapies). And if we want to push the illogic further, as most people do, we can logically derive other distorted beliefs from these basic three "musts." For example, assuming that I must always be competent, if I fail at a task, I can either infer that I am a very bad person or that I will never be competent or both.

Whether Ellis's list of three basic, all encompassing distortions is indeed complete (and therefore logical) is debatable. As noted in Chapter Two, a focus on what Ellis calls "musturbation" may place too little emphasis on fear, anger, and sadness, although Ellis's subordinate references to needing the "approval of others" or concern about "unfairness" take us, respectively, to the second emotion (in this case, fear of what other people think) and the third emotion (a concern for "fairness" lies at the heart of anger). Ellis's view that "musturbations" (desires) act as a special trigger for emotional disturbance is also at variance with the hypothesis of this book that no single emotion underlies all emotional disturbance, that disturbance can theoretically begin in any emotion and then spread into any and all emotions and mental modes.

In some respects, Aaron Beck's brand of "cognitive" therapy is similar to Ellis's, in some respects different. Like Ellis, Beck is semantically oriented. He listens intently to what his patients say and attempts to catch the underlying "errors" of unfactuality and illogic. He and his followers look for categories of unfactual and illogical thinking, although the categories describe certain *kinds* of thoughts, rather than the actual thoughts themselves, and include examples such as "all-or-nothing thinking" (if I'm not perfect, I am a total failure), overgeneralizing (one failure means I will always fail), mind reading (I assume that others are thinking critical thoughts about me with no real evidence for it), and "should or must" statements (like Ellis's), among others. Each of these types of distortions is both unfactual and illogical (for example, all-or-nothing thinking both excludes some relevant factual data and violates the completeness rule of logic), and it is one of Beck's contributions to emphasize that so many distorted statements are both unfactual and illogical at the same time.

Beck is also like Ellis in that in addition to stressing the value of factual and logical thinking, he also stresses the benefits of action. Because emotions and behavior are so closely tied together, it is not enough to think factual and logical thoughts, it is essential to act on them as well. Only by constantly repeating the constructive actions that flow out of factual and logical thinking (for example, getting out of bed and looking for a job when unemployed) can we imprint the habit of being factual and logical on a reliable basis. Finally, both Ellis and Beck inject a purely emotive element into their primarily logico-empirical therapy (in Ellis's case it is included in the name rational-emotive therapy), but they go about it differently. An Ellis-trained therapist may be a bit pushy, bossy, or authoritarian with the patient, as Ellis often is. If the patient strays in his or her thinking, he or she may be chewed out on the spot. A Beck-trained therapist would usually be empathetic and less directive. He or she is a supportive and even loving coach, not a stern parent figure.

It is sometimes objected that cognitive therapies throw out the baby with the bathwater by killing emotion, not just reforming it, but there is no evidence to support this. If logico-empirical approaches help us find the fifth emotion, our emotions need be no less intense or vibrant for that. Another objection is that cognitivists knock down people's habitual ways of living as unfactual or illogical without supplying new goals to fill the vacuum, other than the rather bloodless goal of living more factually and logically. A third more technical objection is that the cognitivists rely on a great deal of grating jargon, along with a long and hard-to-remember series of little self-help exercises, or, more seriously, that both Ellis and Beck sometimes seem to confuse the various emotional states (as when Ellis ascribes all problems to "musturbation" or Beck's colleague David Burns suggests that perfectionism [a particular strategy of the first emotion, desire] stems from fear without offering any real evidence for this).

Not surprisingly, being human, cognitivists will from time to time make an unfactual statement or fall into a minor logical fallacy. For example, David Burns states unqualifiedly in his book *Feeling Good* that "we don't die if we make mistakes"[26] and "there is no such thing as a bad mother,"[27] whereas most of us can think of instances where people have died from their mistakes, and most of us can think of individuals who would fit a commonly accepted definition of "bad" mother, for example one who is physically abusive. Burns also sometimes speculates about a patient's background or childhood and then assumes the speculation to be a fact, or states that such and such (doing well on a test) has nothing to do with your "worth as a human being,[28] when no factual comment can be made about a purely emotive concept such as "worth." Sometimes the problem is logical; e.g., failure to distinguish between an extreme devotion to alcohol or work, labeling both an addiction. Similarly, Burns's statement that "abstract labels such as 'worth-less' or 'inferior' communicate nothing and mean nothing" repeats the logical error committed by the early logical positivists and corrected by the philosopher Charles Stevenson, because words of this type communicate emotions, and emotions do communicate something and mean something, even if that something does not happen to be factual or logical. When cognitivists stretch the facts or stray a bit from logic, it is usually because that seems helpful to the patient, but this in turn can lead to the charge, presumably unfair, that the cognitivists are just sophists, people who claim to believe in fact and logic but who will make any argument to move the patient toward change.

If cognitivists have a real failing, it is probably in their desire to offer themselves as scientific, in their failure to realize that, in addition to a technique, they are really offering a value system, or in other words a kind of religion, either a refined religion of factuality and logic or a more popular religion (in Ellis's case, of "eat, love, and have sex;" * in Beck's or Burns's case, either of "cost-benefit analysis"[30] or of what philosopher William James called positivistic "healthy-mindedness"). It is all very well, and entirely appropriate, to tell patients they are being unfactual or illogical, and that it is making them unnecessarily manic, fearful, angry, or gloomy, but opting for factuality or logic is a value choice, a fact that cognitivists understandably skip over lightly. It should not be surprising that a therapist, confronted with a confused and emotionally upset patient, would prefer to offer a series of "scientific" techniques in a society that glorifies science, and not readily acknowledge that what is really being offered is a philosophy of life, perhaps a philosophy of life well suited for the patient but nevertheless essentially a choice about personal values.

Indirect approach four: Changing emotions through intuition

Like changing our emotions through logic, this notion of changing our emotions through intuition may initially seem far-fetched. After all, when our emotions are agitated, the gentle, barely perceptible voice of our intuitive mind is stilled and cannot be heard over the din. On the

---

* This is what Ellis, in *How To Stubbornly Refuse To Make Yourself Miserable About Anything*, says he would do if he learned life on earth would end in a few days.[29]

other hand, by strengthening our intuitive voice through meditation and other means, it is possible gradually to guide our emotions, to find the fifth emotion, and to stay there most of the time.

Intuition is sometimes described in mystical or metaphysical terms as a "higher" power, but, if so, it is a higher power that we share with at least some other animals. Research with caged chimpanzees has demonstrated that when a chimp is given several sticks, each too short to reach a bunch of bananas invitingly placed just outside the cage, the initial reaction is often to probe with one of the sticks, even though it is clearly too short, and then to exhibit a negative emotional response. After the emotion fades, however, and sometimes after the chimp has turned to other activities, the realization may suddenly dawn that the sticks could be made to fit together end-to-end, and after this intuitive flash, the sticks are then assembled and successfully used to fetch the bananas.[31] For humans too, intuition generally comes to us in the form of a flash of illumination, when our largely unconscious, nonverbal, and thus hidden intuitive powers suddenly penetrate the rigid shell of our conscious mind and give us an answer that can then be "dressed up" for logical or empirical exposition.

Humanity's greatest minds have been highly expert at combining intuition, emotion, logic, and sense experience, but these modes are inherently different and thus always in conflict to one degree or another. From the point of view of a great intuitionist, for example an Indian mystic or Zen Buddhist, logic leads us astray into what the Third Patriarch of Zen called the burdensome practice of judging, of drawing needless distinctions, of separating one thing from another and ourselves from others, when, if we listen to our quiet intuitive voice, it will lead us to reconciliation and unity with the world and others. Similarly, an intuitionist might take sense experience and empiricism to task for its alleged superficiality, its callow certainty that only what we can see, hear, touch, taste, or smell is real, that only the most limited form of consciousness really counts, the related tendency to scan the world around restlessly, without real focus, to waste enormous amounts of energy reacting to the stimulus of every experience, and above all for trying to sell us on the joys of sense experience, of pleasure and novelty, when those joys are sure to fade with age, and soon enough, reveal the worm at the apple's core.

For a dedicated intuitionist, however, emotion poses by far the greatest obstacle. In the first place, as noted above, it deafens us to intuition. In the second place, it propagates and often locks us into empty doctrines and useless dogmas that may lead us into implacable enmity with others. In the third place, and most treacherously, emotion becomes confused with intuition because both have unconscious or semi-conscious roots, and this confusion leads to untold mischief. Traditional psychoanalysis, for example, has equated the unconscious with the emotions, has sought to pull out and express our negative emotions despite psychologist William James's warning, voiced before Freud, that to express a negative emotion is to give it new life, to refuse to express it is to let it die,[32] despite the advice of centuries of sages that it is the gentler and wiser intuitions that need to be brought to light and expressed. How many therapists have told their patients not only to express their emotions, but to trust them, rely on them, glorify them, when it is really the inarticulate but sounder guidance of the intuitions that should be trusted and relied on.

By now, you, the reader, may have noticed something wrong here. In describing how the intuitionist differs from votaries of logic, sense experience, or emotion, we have been drawing distinctions, we have been doing what logicians do and true intuitionists rarely do. Yes, intuition-ists are aware of these distinctions. But they pay them little heed. Logic, empiricism, and emotion all have a place, they say, all should be welcomed in the mind, all should be released when the mind is ready to let them go. Modes of mental activity, like all the other categories we create, are merely chimeras, sometimes useful, often not, in the swirling, vibrating, far from solid, changing, dreamlike world in which all of us actually live according to science as well as according to ancient intuitions.

In similar fashion, intuitionists would not usually speak of therapies, of tools that can be used to dislodge unwanted emotions or emotion-al values, since the words "therapy" and "tool" tend to be associated with the superficially reductionist world of sense experience. They would instead speak of practices or skills to be learned, intuitive practices or skills that are worthwhile in themselves but that also loosen knotted emotions and open the way for changes in one's life. Among these skills is humor, a sense of the absurd that wells up from our intuition and is far removed from the weighty and serious precincts of logic, empiricism, or emotion. What humor gives us above all is detachment, which is the single best key to finding our inner well-springs of intuition. In practice, this may mean something as simple as giving a chronically quarreling couple two squirt guns to shoot at each other or relearning the childhood gift of allowing oneself to be utterly silly and unselfconscious in the presence of others.

Another related intuitionist practice or skill is paradox. For example, individuals coming to an intuitionist counselor expressing a desire to change may be told that they should instead concentrate on accepting themselves as they are. As Swami Ajaya explains: "This approach is the antithesis of how the personal self functions, and it is the key to transcending identification with the personal self and its inherent dis-ease. Paradoxically, acceptance of what is opens the door to change—not the change intended by the personal self, but change that flows effortlessly when we release ourselves from the posture of trying and efforting." *[33]

Psychiatrist Viktor Frankl has combined humor and paradox explicitly in what he calls paradoxical

---

* Not accepting ourselves also usually leads to a plethora of excuses. If I habitually avoid confrontations with others, even necessary ones such as asking for a raise, it is because I am "high strung" or some other excuse. If I just accept my failings, I can dispense with the excuses and start changing.

intention: a patient who cannot stop smoking is told to encourage himself to smoke constantly, a businessman who is always petrified before giving a speech is instructed to tell himself to be as nervous as possible, a mother who cannot stop interfering in the lives of her adult children is told to coach herself to think of more ways to interfere, and in each case it has the desirable reverse effect. Paradoxical intention works in part because it appeals to the patient's sense of humor and thus lightens the "this is so heavy" feeling; partly because it helps the patient accept himself or herself in the manner prescribed by Swami Ajaya; in part, because it brings the emotion to full consciousness, where it dissolves; in part, because it reminds us that, after all, we are not so out of control that we cannot make choices about our moods and actions.

Another intuitionist practice or skill is concentration, either concentration on something outside us or inside us. For example, Thoreau describes the effect of temporarily leaving the world of people to live in the midst of and closely observe nature in the woods around Walden Pond: "A few weeks after I came to the woods, for an hour I doubted whether the near neighborhood of man was not essential to a serene and healthy life. To be alone was somewhat unpleasant. But, in the midst of a gentle rain, while these thoughts prevailed, I was suddenly sensible of such sweet and beneficent society in Nature, in the very pattering of the drops, and in every sight and sound around my house, an infinite and unaccountable friendliness all at once. . . . Every little pine-needle expanded and swelled with sympathy and befriended me. I was so distinctly made aware of the presence of something kindred to me, that I thought no place could ever be strange to me again."[34]

Most intuitionist practices and skills are exceedingly simple, perhaps deceptively so, in that they can take years to master, but simple all the same. S. N. Goenka's Vipassana Buddhism, for example, which as faithfully as possible restores and follows the Buddha's own example and which has inspired a technique known as "mindfulness" taught at the University of Massachusetts Medical School and elsewhere, has us simply concentrate on our own breath ("the breath is your anchor")[35] and then by extension on each of our bodily sensations. As we observe our breath and our bodily sensations, in itself an empirical technique but much more focused than our empirical mind usually permits, we try not to react (if we do react, our breath will tell us by becoming "rough").[36] Nor would Goenka even insist on this particular form of interior concentration. If we wish to substitute prayer or some other technique, that is fine. Whatever the specific regimen of daily quiet, concentration, and practice, if we follow this regimen faithfully, not only will our intuitive powers be strengthened; in addition, the emotional part of our mind should eventually shift back into the fifth emotion, from which position emotional and other changes will come naturally, even effortlessly.

9. Direct Therapies

In the language of this book, a direct path to changing our emotions means using our emotions to fix our emotions rather than relying on logic, sense experience, or intuition to get us out of whatever emotional dead-ends we may have wandered into. This may sound simple and easy; it is anything but.

As previously noted, the purpose of emotions appears to be both to connect and disconnect us to the world and to other people. Since we depend on other people for survival as well as psychic comfort, connection must be at least as important, and arguably much more important, than disconnection. And since living habitually in desire, fear, anger, and sadness keeps disconnecting us, the key emotional therapeutic technique is to keep trying to make enduring connections, to stay involved with the world, to be with other people, to learn from emotional trial and error, however painful and however long it takes. On one level, life makes this approach inescapable, because we cannot really evade the world and are always surrounded by other people. But because desire, fear, anger, and sadness keep separating us from the world and others, keep driving us into a willful, fearful, defiant, or sad isolation, it often requires considerable fortitude and determination. At the roughest points, it will always seem easier simply to accept isolation, whether the overt isolation of a fearful escapist or depressed shut-in or the de facto isolation of a desire-drenched con man or angry tyrant.

If the direct path to the fifth emotion lies in getting "on-the-job" training in the sometimes daunting task of connecting emotionally with the world and others, there are several different ways of setting out down this path, each of which is worth briefly enumerating, although they will be familiar to all.

Direct approach one: Change emotions by trying to connect with one other person

If we can create a successful emotional connection with one person, we can probably go on to make a multitude of successful connections. Finding such a person, however, may be difficult. Assuming that we have not alienated all of our friends, coaches, mentors or family members, we could turn to one of these or to a professional therapist. For this approach to work, however, the friend, spouse, or therapist must live largely in the fifth emotion, and how can we—perennially stuck as we are—possibly distinguish someone who does? So there must be a considerable element of luck. Beyond that, if we are really lucky, the other party will show us what psychologist Carl Rogers called "unconditional positive regard," a degree of acceptance that transcends all the inevitable short-term conflicts, and will, in general, abstain from overtly judging us or directly telling us what to do. As Rogers has written: "In my relationships with [clients] my aim has been to provide a climate which contains as much of safety, of warmth, of empathic understanding, as I can genuinely find in myself to give. I have not found it satisfying or helpful to intervene in the client's experience with diagnostic or interpretive explanations, nor with suggestions and guidance."[1] Rogers' idea of "unconditional positive regard" as a precondition for emotional change has been widely accepted and works well both within and without therapy; that is, a friend, spouse, or therapist can apply it with equally good results. The related idea of nondirectiveness has proved more problematical. An undirected therapy may seem aimless, time-consuming, and prohibitively expensive, something really only available for the rich. On the other hand, a friend or spouse will almost never change a loved one by being directive, much less bossy, and will only ignore Rogers' advice at his or her peril.

Direct approach two: Change emotions by trying to connect with a group of people who come together for the specific purpose of supporting each other emotionally

This approach was also pioneered by Carl Rogers, among others, and has continued to flourish in psychologist Scott Peck's "community building workshops" and poet and author Robert Bly's "wild man" weekends in the woods. The actual techniques vary, but in Scott Peck's workshops, a group of people, often strangers, come together for a few days of largely undirected discussion with each other, pass through the usual preliminaries of superficial politeness, followed by conflict and increasing "chaos," interrupted by one or more members of the group proving to be in emotional crisis, and thus desperately needing the group's support, followed by a period of emptying-out or silence, followed in most cases, as a phoenix out of the ashes, by a wave of mutual empathy and emotional reconciliation (the equivalent of what William James called "melting moods"[2]), climaxed with much hugging and general good feeling all round. As one participant recalled, "I experienced [a] healing warmth and safety . . . a hundred times more intense [than ever before]. I was humbled and grateful beyond words. I knew my life would never be the same."[3]

Underlying all such gatherings, regardless of the specific form they take, are a few basic premises, each of them controversial. The first is that all of us are emotionally "damaged," whatever facade we may erect, that we all need, in the words of a contributor to Ann Landers' column, to find people "to talk to, cry with and even scream at....Most of all, [we need people] to hold [us] and tell [us] that everything [is] going to be better [because] after all, these [are] the basic needs of all hurting people."*[4] The second premise,

* Although this is too dramatic for many people's taste, one should remember biologist Jane Goodall's comment about the African chimpanzees she has studied for decades: It is "impossible to overemphasize the importance of friendly

even more controversial than the first, is that we should go outside the immediate circle of family and close friends to find other people with whom we can share our most intimate emotions. The third premise, most controversial of all, is that, as an alternative to establishing more-or-less ongoing emotional support groups, we can accomplish the same objectives by coming together and sharing emotionally with strangers for a weekend, even though, or even because, we will probably never see them again. This latter approach has been dismissed by some critics as emotional "promiscuity," but whether this is a fair characterization or not, Peck acknowledges that community-building workshops often tend to unleash sexual as well as other energies.

Direct approach three: Change emotions by trying to connect with a group of people united by a common, continuing purpose

The obvious paradigm here is a family, a set of people making a life together and perhaps raising children. Obviously there is no better preparation for a life predominantly lived in the fifth emotion than to be born and grow up in a family that predominantly lives in that emotion. Even then, of course, the children may turn out to be the proverbial "apples falling far from the tree." Alternatively, the parents may be predominantly

---

physical contact for the well-being of the chimpanzee. Again and again one can watch a frightened or tense individual relax if she is patted, kissed or embraced reassuringly by a companion." *New York Times Magazine,* May 17, 1987, p. 110.

angry and abusive, predominantly over-demanding and controlling, predominantly fearful, withdrawn, and neglectful, or predominantly sad, clinging, and dependent, and the children may respond with more of the same.

Even if one's immediate family fails to nourish and sustain fifth emotion values, there are sometimes other, family-like groups where one can experience or experiment with the fifth emotion. By most accounts, President Franklin Roosevelt did not have a happy family life, either as a child or as an adult, but while President he became very attached to a small "family" of close aides who shared his work, some of whom even moved into the White House; and he had his fellow "polios" (victims of polio, like himself), whom he organized into an extensive support group centering on a shared rehabilitation center in Warm Springs, Georgia. Warm Springs was a sunny, happy place where everybody helped everybody else, where the patients, not the doctors, were in charge, where Roosevelt and others picnicked, partied, sang, swam, and generally enjoyed themselves no matter how severe the physical handicap to be overcome.

FDR's Warm Springs was in many respects a precursor of the thousands of support groups that have proliferated in our own time, some organized around shared illnesses such as cancer, others like Alcoholics Anonymous and its myriad offshoots organized around emotional and behavioral as well as medical problems. But support groups need not be organized around anything and can arise quite spontaneously whenever people share a life and show some concern for each other. Roosevelt's distant cousin Joseph Alsop describes in his memoirs how his first several years at boarding school were "grim," "lonely," and "desolate." At length it dawned on him that "other young people like to make friends, although friendship, on the whole, requires effort. . . . In the main, sociability is a knack; but it is also partly a skill, to be learned and cultivated like any other. Therefore, friendship returned is almost invariably equal to friendship given. Over the years, assiduous attention to this rule has . . . provided me with a long and rich vein of sustenance and security. . . . "[5] Ann Landers captured the same sentiment even more succinctly when she wrote in her column that "there are the 'givers' and then there are the 'takers.' The 'takers' don't know what they are missing. I can tell them— they're missing the best part of living."[6]

Direct approach four: Change emotions by trying to connect with a group of people united by a common, continuing purpose that is larger than themselves

In most cases, it is somewhat arbitrary to say whether a group is focused inwardly, like a family, on itself, or outwardly, like a surgical team, on a mission larger than itself. Every group, to some degree, is focused both on itself and on some larger mission. Roosevelt's "polios" were helping each other at Warm Springs, and thus focused inwardly, but they were also showing the world that polio victims could rehabilitate their muscles, recapture the joy of living, and lead purposeful lives. Drug addicts, meeting in self-help groups, are similarly pointing the way for other addicts, and so forth.

On the other hand, some groups are much more outwardly focused than others. One does not join Mother Teresa's order of nuns in order to minister to the needs of other nuns, but rather to minister to the needs of the poor, especially the dying poor and orphans, and experience of such a group cannot help but affect our emotional values deeply. On a more secular level, if we join environmental groups, we may have some slight hope of saving our planet's air or water or forests for ourselves, but we are more likely concerned about saving it for others, especially future generations. And if we join the French resistance during the Nazi occupation, we may be fiercely attached to our compatriots, but think nothing of thrusting both them and ourselves into mortal danger.

When we not only join a cause that feels larger than ourselves, but fervently embrace it, personal change is almost certain to follow. As William James observed, "hope, happiness, security, resolve, emotions characteristic of conversion, can be ... explosive. And emotions that come in this explosive way seldom leave things as they found them."[7] Although this process may ultimately prove disappointing, we have Saint Paul's example of a conversion that did not simply rechannel the old hate or the old sorrow, and there is no lack of examples in today's world as well. As Ron Webeck, an AIDS sufferer who chose to transcend AIDS, has said: "What keeps me alive is the feeling that I can't let other people down. The more people I help, the better I get."[8]

Direct approach five: Adopt a goal that transcends oneself

This approach is superficially different than those which went before because one does not initially try to join a group. One instead defines a goal or mission that is both self-transcending and truly moves us, that is, moves our emotions, so that our emotions become intensely attached to it. For example, the goal might be to learn science in order to find a cure for a disease or to develop a way to teach dyslexic children to read. What happens, of course, is that no matter how solitary the goal may seem at first (e.g., long hours in a laboratory or at home writing a book), if it is truly self-transcending, it will eventually bring us back into contact with people and enroll us with groups of people sharing the goal in some way.

Unlike in the examples given above, the particular goals or missions chosen may be extremely humble, and we may find that they have chosen us rather than our choosing them. Psychiatrist Viktor Frankl, whose central therapy, called "logotherapy," reflects the idea that having an emotional mission or purpose is all-important, tells how a grieving widower came to him in a state of extreme sadness. Frankl asked the man how his wife would have reacted if he, rather than she, had died, if she, rather than he, had had to carry on bereaved and alone. In a sense, had he not, by continuing to live, spared her great pain, and was this not the meaning imbedded in his own pain? The man responded to this advice with great relief because it not only gave him a sense of purpose; it also made him feel closer to the beloved wife he had lost.

Direct approach six: Combine any of the five previous approaches with physical activity

The emotional component of our brain is concerned with activities. It wants us to join in joyously with others, or, conversely, to grab, flee, fight, or capitulate, as our most primitive urgings and the occasion seem to demand. As a result, the emotional brain seems to change most readily when it is active. For example, if my friend and I want to stop smoking, we may be more successful if we first take up jogging or weight-lifting together. If another close friend has lapsed into despondency over a diagnosis of cancer, I may be able to help coax him or her back to the fifth emotion, which among other things should improve immune function, simply by listening, by offering a human connection, but I may accomplish more if in addition I lure him or her into an outdoor game such as tennis, or better still, sign both of us up for a doubles tournament. Similarly, if I want to tutor a teenager living in a ghetto, I may be more successful if I start each tutoring session with a lesson in oriental martial arts or with some vigorous basketball lay-ups. And if I want to create an emotional connection between strangers quickly, I can either follow psychiatrist

Scott Peck's techniques (as described under Approach Two) or I can lead the group into the wilderness to hike, mountain climb, kayak, and learn survival skills together (as Outward Bound does). Either of these approaches may produce the desired result, as Scott Peck has himself noted,[9] but if I can somehow combine the two, the odds for success will be even greater.

When one participates in an Outward Bound experience, the outdoor, physical challenges are chosen and, therefore, to some degree controlled. When we face unexpected and unchosen physical challenges, especially with others, the emotional effect can be even greater, as it was on Franklin Roosevelt when he contracted polio or on Joseph Alsop when he suddenly found himself in a Japanese prisoner of war camp during World War Two. Physical challenges need not be so extreme, however, in order to achieve a profound effect on our sense of emotional connection or disconnection with the world. Film star Robert Patrick (*Terminator 2*) tells how he quit college and drifted ("I didn't like myself at all. Something was eating at me"[10]) until one day he, his brother, and four friends found themselves trying to stay afloat in the middle of Lake Erie after their boat had capsized in a storm. Patrick had the only life preserver and used it to swim three hours to shore while his companions clung to the hull. The group was eventually rescued, but for Patrick it was an important epiphany, a moment in which he connected with others, shared a purpose larger than himself, the survival of his group, and ultimately reconnected with life itself. As he swam through heavy swells, uncertain of his or his companions' fate, he repeated: "I'll quit wasting my life."[11]

As indicated above, emotion is naturally active, so we learn emotional lessons better when active, especially when active and under stress. Logic, empiricism, and intuition may also be combined with action, but then the challenge becomes to protect these mental modes from the emotional intrusion that activity brings. Masters of logic, empiricism, or intuition become extremely adept at operating on several mental levels at the same time, as when Mohandas Gandhi maintained his intuitive calm, humor, and detachment whether surrounded by enemies or by millions of admirers, whether in contemplation at home or traveling for weeks in open train cars.

Caveats

As noted at the beginning of this chapter, the direct approach to changing our emotional values—that is, the approach of learning through trial and error, through our everyday efforts to form an attachment to at least one other human being—has the great advantage of being inescapable, since we are tribal creatures who must necessarily try to get along with one another, and may be the best or even the only possible therapy for a particular individual, for example an individual who is especially emotional, and not so inclined to look at matters logically, empirically, or intuitively. As psychiatrist Viktor Frankl pointed out,[12] people are not satisfied simply to be happy, and rarely succeed at being happy, if they make that their primary goal. Rather, people want a reason to be happy, a sense of meaning in their life, which is only supplied by a sense of values, and membership in a group immediately supplies something or someone to value, nourish, and protect at the most basic emotional level. That said, the natural human search for a tribal connection is not without its potential pitfalls, a few of which should be briefly enumerated:

♦ If we make the wrong connection, we may reinforce our old emotional values rather than find new ones. Two demanding perfectionists, for example, may find each other, marry, and live in a cocoon of mutually reinforcing perfectionism, notwithstanding all the suffering it brings, for the rest of their lives.

♦ By joining a new group, we may loosen one undesirable emotion, such as an obsession with alcohol (desire), but simultaneously protect an even stronger undesirable emotion, such as a compulsive need for attention (also desire). For example, columnist Colman McCarthy has asked why celebrity addicts leave treatment centers and immediately plunge into a round of television interviews. As he notes, "their quasi-normalcy [after treatment] poorly masks that they are still addicted—to applause. . . . A high is a high, whether from drugs, dirty phone calls or cheers from the crowds. . . ."[13]

♦ Instead of relinquishing one undesirable emotion, and in the process reinforcing another, we may instead simply substitute one undesirable emotion for another. For example, some alcoholics on joining Alcoholics Anonymous may become as obsessed with their group or the recovery process as they previously were with alcohol.

♦ Through group membership, we may not only reinforce old values; we may magnify them as well. It is doubtful that the guards at the Nazi death camps would have been as angrily sadistic or would have acted out their sadism so savagely if they had not been part of the Nazi machinery.

♦ As briefly noted in Chapter Four, the "us" element of a group, the very glue that connects its members, often creates a "them," a sense of outsiders who are not part of a group. This may be acceptable when the "us" is a research staff and the "them" is a disease-causing virus or bacterium. But when the "us" versus "them" is mixed with fearful and angry emotions of paranoia and hatred, outsiders may become completely dehumanized. Thus, Baruch Goldstein, a doctor from Brooklyn, New York, who gunned down thirty Arabs as they prayed at a mosque in Hebron, justified himself by saying that "the Arabs are the Nazis [of today]. . . . Anybody who acts to support the Jewish people in the end will be rewarded; anybody who acts against the

Jewish people in the end will be punished. That's a promise [of] God."[14] In a similar vein, a self-described "chaplain" of a "militia" allegedly linked to Timothy McVeigh, convicted of mass murder in blowing up the Federal Office Building in Oklahoma City, described McVeigh as "a good guy ... the kind of guy who forms allegiances to the death."[15] On an imaginary but still disturbing level, a radical feminist novel refers to all men as "rapists" and justifies random street killings of men for "vengeance."[16] And on a considerably less lurid note, thousands of self-help groups centered on a concept of being adult children (e.g., children of alcoholics) have sprung up in the United States and, in many cases, have glued together their participants by turning parents into a kind of enemy. As advice columnist Ann Landers has observed about this: "Telling people their parents damaged them serves no useful purpose. Placing the blame [anger] is always counterproductive."[17]

♦ Because groups both join us with those in the group and separate us from those outside, and because groups can intensify and magnify our emotions, minor differences with others may be blown entirely out of proportion, and in the process we can completely lose touch with our sense of humor (intuition) or our empirical or logical reasoning facilities. For example, it is frequently observed that in the United States, political and social conflicts and decisions often revolve around the concept of race, while in Europe they more commonly revolve around the concept of ethnicity or class. Yet none of these concepts has any clear and measurable scientific basis. With respect to race, there is no scientific way to define an exact point where "white" becomes "black" or vice versa. We could just as logically decide that body shape or eye color is the "important" defining characteristic of Americans, rather than race, and start asking for that data in census surveys, and make it the basis of political or social policy.

♦ Some groups merely mask the desire of one individual, the so-called leader, to exercise power and authority by thrusting his or her values upon others. Often this is done under false, or at least misguided, pretenses. For example, in the hands of an unscrupulous or self-deceiving religious leader, the teachings of Jesus can be reinterpreted and transvalued into a sad masochism (I am the most pitiful and hopeless sinner), conjoined with a desire driven grandiosity (as a true Christian I am better than others), a fearful paranoia (anti-Christians are trying to destroy our religion and nation), and an angry hatred (our enemies must be destroyed and punished). In many instances, group (or cult) leaders will use variations on standard brainwashing techniques, a mild example of which is to subject people to stress (e.g., forbidding use of toilets during an all-day harangue), then lift the stress and suggest that the resulting mood improvement is attributable to the program. This particular technique is as old as humanity, as suggested by the Russian folk tale of the peasant who approaches his priest and complains that he is so depressed he plans to take his life. The priest advises the peasant to take his cows and goats into his house for two weeks, then put them back in their stalls and return. When he does return, the peasant affirms that he feels much better.

10. Integrating the Two

🔥 First, we will try to summarize, in the following diagrams, where we have been:

I. THE INDIRECT APPROACH			
(Relying on nonemotive techniques to change our emotions)			
A. *Rely on logic*	**B.** *Rely on sense experience*	**C.** *Rely on combination of A. & B. (Logico-empirical techniques)*	**D.** *Rely on intuition*
Socratic method Milton Erickson Any therapy that distinguishes, differentiates, classifies, or applies order, organization, consistency, clarity, relevance, and completeness tests to values and behavior	Behavioral therapies Any therapy involving observation, immersion, or distraction	Karen Horney (partly) Cognitive therapy (Aaron Beck) Rational/emotive therapy (Albert Ellis)	Humor Paradox Paradoxical intention (Viktor Frankl) Concentration (e.g., Henry Thoreau) Yoga Vipassana Buddhism "Mindfulness"

II. THE DIRECT APPROACH
(Relying on emotion itself to change our emotions)

A. Enter into relationship with one person	**B.** Enter into relationship with a group in passing	**C.** Combination of A. & B.	**D.** Enter into relationship with an on-going group
Close friendship Freudian-based psychoanalysis Jungian analysis Carl Rogers' client-centered therapy Cognitive therapy Rational/ emotive therapy (partly)	Carl Rogers' (partly) Scott Peck's community building	"Humanistic" therapies Gestalt	Family Family therapy School Job Group therapy such as psychodynamic Alcoholics Anonymous and similar self-help or addiction recovery groups Other support groups

E. Enter into relationship with a group seeking to transcend itself	**F.** Connect with a self-transcending emotional goal (which, if initially solitary, will even-tually connect us to others)	**G.** Any of A. through D. combined with physical activity	
Mother Teresa's order of nuns The French resistance during W.W.II Greenpeace The Christian Coalition	Logo-therapy (Viktor Frankl)	Bio-energetics Outward Bound Counseling with sports or martial arts Counseling with massage therapy	Counseling with Hatha Yoga, breathing, or Tai Chi Counseling with other relaxation or movement techniques

Legitimacy of various therapies

Is one of these approaches or therapies better than another? Before even trying to answer this question, we had better assure ourselves that the therapies are indeed what they claim, not innocent or nefarious covers for something different. For example, traditional Freudian therapy claimed for decades that it was in some sense scientific, at the very least rooted in logic or sense experience—a claim that it never lived up to, which is why it is listed above as an emotive technique. As psychiatrist Viktor Frankl pointed out, Freudian psycho-analysis, in addition to being an emotive technique, also represents a particular emotional attitude: one which looks for hidden and usually sinister motives, delights in debunking and devaluing, and in many ways exhibits a subtly angry persona. Contrariwise, therapies may not be deceptive in and of themselves but may be twisted and distorted to suit the purposes of an aggrandizing individual. For example, according to a number of former practitioners, a well-known brand of self-described "neo-cognitive therapy" is not about cognitive therapy at all, but rather a mask for the fund-raising and power-seeking of an authoritarian cult leader.

Valuing the various therapies

Having assured ourselves of the bona fides of the therapies listed above, the question remains whether one broad approach or one therapy will help more than another. To put this in a specific context, let us consider the case of a 32-year-old male who writes to advice columnist Ann

Landers that he is still a virgin, "quick-tempered and just plain rotten to be around" [anger], certain "no woman would be interested" in him despite his good job [sadness], "self-conscious" [fear], and "frustrated about his inability to have a physical relationship" [desire].[1] Will logic help this young man? Or sense experience? Or intuition? Will one of the direct emotional therapies work best? The world is full of opinions about this. A therapist writes that "feelings are the truth," thus seemingly excluding any role for logic or empiricism. A letter-writer to *Newsweek* states that alcoholics or other recovering addicts who try to think through their problem "are attempting to use the thing that failed them to begin with—their brains, [an approach] AA knows [to be] futile."[2] An intuitionist might argue that the young man is so alienated from others, especially women, because he is too critical, too quick to see differences, too logical, while a logician such as Joshua Halberstam might counter that "wisdom is the ability to make distinctions"[3] and thus take one problem at a time. A therapist of the rational-emotive school, speaking to a workshop in Washington, D.C., states that "the most important variable in behavior change is forcing yourself to behave differently than you feel"[4] (i.e. the young man should try to be nice and ask women out, no matter what he is feeling), while Karen Horney maintains the old-fashioned view that we cannot necessarily expect feelings to change with behavior.[5] *

---

* I believe that on this issue Horney is less correct.

With so many discordant voices, it would
seem very difficult to choose among them, but
fortunately it may not even be necessary. As
previously noted, the logical, empirical, intuitive, and emotional spheres of our brain are so
closely interconnected that change anywhere
will as a general rule produce change elsewhere, a sharpening of our logical thinking will
help us in our emotions, and vice versa.
Moreover, it may not matter that much where
we start. As the 19th century philosopher and
theologian John Cardinal Newman wrote in a
sermon: the mind "passes on from point to
point, gaining one by some indication; another
on a probability; then availing itself of an
association; then falling back on some received
law; next seizing on testimony; then commit-
ting itself to some popular impression, or some
inward instinct, or some obscure memory; and
thus it makes progress not unlike a clamberer
on a steep cliff, who, by quick eye, prompt
hand, and firm foot, ascends how he knows not
himself. . . ."[6]

Values of the various therapies

To say, however, that we could be helped by
any of these approaches, in any order, is not to
say that we would be equally receptive to
them. As we have already noted, each of these
therapies embodies not only a technique, but
also a series of value judgments, both about the
technique and about life in general, or in other
words embodies a value system. Albert Ellis,
the founder of rational/emotive therapy, readily

acknowledges that his therapy is based not only on certain assumptions about what is most valuable methodologically (viz., logic and sense experience followed by emotional empathy), but also on what matters most in life (for him, survival, pleasure, and happiness,[7] which together express a familiar form of philosophical utilitarianism), and every other therapy is equally value-loaded. As a general rule, then, we will tend to be more receptive to a therapy if there is something about its values that already makes us feel some kinship toward it.

Sometimes the nature of the kinship may not be readily apparent. What was it, for example, about the values of Saul of Tarsus that predisposed him to make the leap to stop persecuting Christians, to embrace Jesus instead, to become Saint Paul? We will never know. But even in such a famous reversal of values, the ground must have been sown, there must have been preexisting values that led Saul to reverse himself. On a much more prosaic level, there might appear to be an unbridgeable chasm between Albert Ellis, the apostle of an uncensored and unconstrained sexuality, and Ann Landers' 32-year-old male virgin—surely the latter would find the former an unsympathetic therapist. But if the young man highly esteems logic and sense experience and if he agrees with Ellis that pleasure is an ultimate goal of life (unlike, say psychiatrist Viktor Frankl or philosopher Robert Nozick, each of whom believes that pleasure is always a by-product of other goals, or, as Nozick puts it, "rides piggyback on other things"[8]), then the unwilling young ascetic might find the older sybarite to be the ideal tutor.

In some instances, people seem so predisposed to one therapeutic approach that an alternative approach seems hardly conceivable, or at least seems hardly conceivable in retrospect. After reading Spinoza, with his formal arguments and proofs, it is hard to imagine him ordering his emotions through any device other than logic, and it is not surprising to hear his sincere dismissal of other methods: "One might perhaps expect [emotive methods of controlling our emotions such as participating in organized religion, feeling contrition and repentance] to help bring . . . [us to] the right path, and might therefore conclude (as everyone does conclude) that these [emotive methods] are good things. Yet when we look at the matter closely, we shall find that not only are they not good, but on the contrary deleterious and evil."[9] Similarly, when a woman writes Ann Landers and states that for twenty years she has controlled her tendency to drink too much by forbidding herself any food for twenty-four hours after she has had a third drink, one guesses that this behaviorist (and therefore empirical) technique is exactly right for this individual, that no other technique would fit her values (and therefore work) as well—even though it is also true, as Ann Landers points out, that such a severe technique might not work so well for "the average mortal."[10]

The "therapy" implicit in this book

Within this context, it is perhaps worth noting, as a natural and inescapable fact, that the entire approach taken in this book, both in its methodology and in the values underlying that methodology, will have appealed to some readers and not to others, will have echoed the personal values of some readers and not others. For example, it should be clear that this author values sense experience (empiricism), because he enjoys observing human beings and their reactions closely, and that he especially values logic, because he has devoted this book to distinguishing, counting, and cataloguing emotions and value systems, each of which is a logical technique, but that he also values emotion in general, and the fifth emotion in particular, very highly since he has taken the trouble to write about it. Moreover, it should be apparent that this book can and should be used normatively by anyone who is attracted to the underlying values and wishes to use the "therapy" that is implicit in it. Indeed, defined in this very loose way, a potential "therapy" is arguably implicit in any philosophical or psychological investigation or hypothesis.

Value the fifth emotion

So what is the "therapy" implicit in this book, or in other words, what is a more explicit version of it? In the first place, this "therapy" argues that if one wants to find and live in the fifth emotion, one should start by making a conscious decision and keep making a conscious decision to value it, which is a logical and thus an "indirect" approach. As we have seen, many people want the fifth emotion, or think they want it, but have reservations: "If I really value happiness, perhaps I will become ordinary" (controlling emotion of desire), "perhaps I will lose my fighting edge" (controlling emotion of anger), "perhaps I will collapse and become more miserable than ever" (controlling emotions of fear and sadness), all of which are not true but may cause alarm. Further, people may be afraid of change (controlling emotion of fear), of having to make certain specific sacrifices, especially sacrifices of desire or hate, but sometimes even of fear or sadness, because they have relied on these emotions and experienced them intensely, and both the reliance and intensity make them meaningful and hard to give up. At the same time—and equally importantly—valuing the fifth emotion does not mean desiring it, especially desiring it with intensity, since that would paradoxically rotate the mind back into the first emotion. It is always helpful to remember that the fifth emotion is hypothesized to be simply equilibrium, the default position that we automatically rotate into when we are not valuing desire, fear, anger, or sadness, and is thus always available.

Survey one's emotions and emotional values

If one has decided that the fifth emotion is the particular emotion to be valued most highly and has made a calm and cheerful albeit firm commitment to it—that is, decided that the other basic emotions should not be valued most highly or committed to—one still has to observe oneself, observe and monitor oneself as closely as possible on a regular basis, to see what emotion one is actually experiencing at the moment. This technique is also logical in its reliance on a classification scheme for emotions such as desire, fear, anger, and sadness, as well as highly empirical in its reliance on observation, both of which make it an "indirect approach" in our terms.

Because basic emotions cannot easily be captured by a single word, are indeed essentially nonverbal (it is even hard to remember words when in the full grip of an emotion), it may be easier to visualize than to verbalize them when monitoring oneself. An especially useful mnemonic device for this purpose is to color code each emotion: green for desire, yellow for fear, red for anger, deep blue for sadness, and light blue (or clear as in a clear day) for happiness. It is also possible to adopt an aversive strategy by visualizing the darker emotions as green, yellow, red, or deep blue idols in the shape of serpents, but this is hardly fair to emotions which are, after all, highly appropriate at times and even vital for survival.

Rebut related thoughts

If one self-monitors (not obsessively, but persistently) and finds that the dark emotions are both more present and harder to dispense with than one would prefer, there is every likelihood that one is thinking and probably dwelling on one or more characteristic emotion-linked thoughts. These characteristic thoughts—or variations on them—need to be brought out to the light of day, and through empirical or logical means revealed to be the falsehoods they usually (although not always) are:

- Desire/green: "I demand X, cannot live without it, and have every right to boss* myself and others to get it."
- Fear/yellow: "I worry that I will die if I enter this airplane [or similar] and/or I will 'die' from wounded pride if people think badly of me [or if I think badly of myself]."
- Anger/red: "People are [or the world is] unfair to me and I have every right to criticize, scorn, blame and abuse."
- Sadness/blue: "I have lost something forever and/or feel guilty because I have made unforgivable mistakes."

The key phrases to keep in mind are *demanding* and *bossing*, *worry* and *pride*, *unfair* and *blaming*, and *loss* and *guilt*. At the simplest level, this can be reduced to *demanding, worrying, blaming,* and *guilt*.

Why the implicit "therapy" outlined above may either attract or repel

Valuing the fifth emotion (reducing the valuation placed on the other four) together with self-surveillance and inner rebuttal of mood and associated thought may be enough to rotate the

---

* As noted earlier, bossing is a form that demanding takes with self or others, and itself assumes many guises, including what psychologists call "caretaking"(creating dependency by doing for others what they can and should do for themselves).

mind more and more into the fifth emotion. If not, if the first four emotions still dominate even after patient and persistent practice, then the approach implicit in this book just may not fit a particular individual, or may have to be supplemented with one of the other approaches reviewed. Frankl's logotherapy is particularly recommended, an approach which synthesizes direct and indirect methods, although he did not articulate it in that way.

As noted previously, both logic and empiricism are innate in everybody, so none of the three simple steps outlined above—consciously valuing, monitoring, and rebutting—should seem absolutely foreign to anybody. Nevertheless, many people are deeply uncomfortable with the logical techniques in particular, with distinguishing, differentiating, counting, and cataloging, especially with respect to human thought and behavior, and indeed find the whole process oversimplified, overabstracted, overcritical, or just offensive in some unspecified way. Even individuals who are empirically oriented, but who prefer to distract themselves when they have emotional problems rather than analyze them, may find the general thrust of this book and the three-step "therapy" implicit in it to be irritating or irrelevant.

Seeking a wider vantage point

All of this is inevitable and not such a bad thing. So long as some people feel an affinity for the approach taken, feel that it is speaking to them, that should be enough. Yet, having said that, there is a further possibility, that having used this book, however helpful or unhelpful it seemed, to analyze and understand one's own individual proclivities and values, one might actually try to climb to a higher ground, seek a wider vantage point, that one might seek, however humbly, to transcend one's own cherished viewpoint, even the cherished viewpoint of this book. Since we are all logical, empirical, intuitive, and emotional creatures, however much we may elevate or denigrate different parts of our armamentarium, why should we not at least attempt to bring together all these facets of ourselves, to look at the world, ourselves, and others from multiple perspectives, as much as possible all at the same time, and to try to remain open to what all these perspectives, approaches, and therapies have to teach us?

William James made a similar point when he wrote that "the obvious outcome of our total experience is that the world can be handled according to many systems of ideas, and is so handled by different men, and will each time give some characteristic kind of profit, while at the same time some other kind of profit has to be omitted or postponed. . . . And why, after all, may not the world be so complex as to consist of many [different realities], which we can thus approach in alternation by using different conceptions and assuming different attitudes, just as mathematicians handle the same numerical and spatial facts by geometry . . . , algebra . . . , calculus . . . , and each time come out right."[11] James was specifically hoping to integrate a "religious" and "scientific" outlook, but the same sentiment can be applied to all the various parts of our brains, at the very least including our logic, sense experience, intuition, and emotion, from which, among many other things, both religion and science emerge.

To appreciate the potential for this kind of broader but integrated thinking, one can imagine an athlete executing a perfect dive from a high board during competition. The diver needs logic to drive home the message that the only way to make the perfect dive under pressure is to practice repeatedly, and then to try; sense experience to store the physical memory of all the practice dives and to provide the reassurance that it has been done and can be done again; intuition to create and guard a quiet command center within amidst the clamor; and emotion to charge (but not overcharge) the muscles and tune them for action.

To try to combine these modes all at once (not merely to compromise between or balance them, but truly to combine and integrate them, both consciously and coherently, and preferably not just in order to compete well or to accomplish something, but as an undertaking for its own sake) puts us to what may be the most interesting and most difficult test that we can choose. Moreover, and importantly, this is a test, a challenge, or a goal that is available to anyone, no matter how young or old, wealthy or poor, powerful or powerless, healthy or infirm, favored or disfavored by place, fortune, or circumstance.

Notes

Introduction

1. Jared Diamond, review of *Naturalist*, by Edward O. Wilson, *New York Review of Books* (January 12, 1995): p. 18.

2. William R. Uttal, *The Psychobiology of Mind* (Hilldale, NJ: Lawrence Erlbaum Associates, 1978): p. 343.

3. John Schwartz, "Putting A Certain Face on Emotions," *The Washington Post* (November 8, 1993): p. A-3.

4. Sandra Blakeslee, "Scientist at Work : Joseph LeDoux; Using Rats to Trace Anatomy of Fear, Biology of Evolution," *The New York Times* (November 5, 1996): p. C-1.

5. "Are Anti-depressants Placebos?" *Harvard Mental Health Letter* (March 1993).

6. Sandra Blakeslee, op. cit.

7. Steve Jones, professor of Genetics at University College, London, review of *How The Mind Works* by Steven Pinker, *New York Review of Books* (November 6, 1997): p. 13.

Chapter 1: Basic Emotions

1. Silvan Tomkins, *Affect, Imagery, Consciousness* (New York: Springer, 1962) and with Carroll Izard, *Affect, Cognition & Personality* (New York: Springer, 1965).

2. Carroll E. Izard, *The Psychology of Emotions* (New York: Plenum Press, 1991). This compares to Tomkins's list of eight emotions: surprise, interest,

joy, rage, fear, disgust, shame, and anguish. Also
see Carroll Izard, *The Face of Emotion* (New York:
Plenum Press, 1971) and *Psychological Review* 99
(1992): pp. 561–65 and 100 (1992): pp. 68–90.
Others (e.g., Paul Ekman, Robert Plutchik, Nico
Frijda, Philip Johnson-Laird, Keith Oatley, and Jaak
Panksepp) have somewhat different lists. For an
excellent discussion of these lists and their critics,
see Joseph LeDoux, *The Emotional Brain* (New York:
Simon& Schuster, 1996): Chapter 5, especially
pp. 113–121.

3. *Merriam-Webster's Collegiate Dictionary* (New York:
Merriam Webster, 1995).

4. *Roget's Thesaurus,* 5th Edition, edited by Robert
Chapman (New York: Harper Collins, 1992).

5. Melody Beattie, *Codependent No More* (New York:
Harper & Row, 1987): p. 154.

6. Glenn Frankel, "After the Ordeal, Together Again,"
The Washington Post (September 27, 1991): p. B-2.

Chapter 2: Shifting Gears

1. William James, *The Varieties of Religious Experience*
(New York: Penguin, 1982): p. 148.

2. Antony and Cleopatra Act III, xi, 194.

3. Albert Ellis and Robert Harper, *Guide to Rational
Living* (North Hollywood, CA: Wilshire, 1974): p.
203.

4. Karen Horney, *Our Inner Conflicts* (New York: W.W.
Norton, 1945): pp. 12–13.

Chapter 3: The Fifth Emotion

1. Johnette Howard, "Jansen's Last Moment is
Golden," *The Washington Post* (February 19, 1994):
p. A-16.

2. "The Wit & Wisdom of the Maestro," *Newsweek* 112, no. 10 (September 5, 1988): p. 55.

3. Kevin Sullivan, "At 'Studs' Search, A Different Breed," *The Washington Post* (November 14, 1992): p. D-8.

4. *Forbes* (August 29, 1994).

5. Chuck Conconi, "Personalities," *The Washington Post* (December 11, 1986): p. B-3.

Chapter 4: Conundrums of Choice

1. Daniel Goleman, "Severe Trauma May Damage the Brain as well as the Psyche; Site for Learning and Memory are Smaller in Some Veterans," *The New York Times* (August 1, 1995): p. C-3.

2. Tom Seligson, "We're all given a choice," *Parade Magazine* (March 17, 1991): p. 11.

3. Ellis and Harper, op. cit., p. 174.

4. Betty Catroux, *W,* vol. 22, no. 19, (fall 1993): p. 58.

5. Joel Achenbach, "Drink No Wine After Its Time?" *The Washington Post* (July 24, 1992): p. D-5.

6. Viktor Frankl, *The Doctor and the Soul* (New York: Vintage, 1986): pp. 14–15.

Chapter 6: Emotions, Values, And Actions

1. David Viscott, *The Language of Feelings* (New York: Pocket Books, 1990): p. 142.

2. Robert Nozick, *The Examined Life* (New York: Touchstone Books, 1989): p. 91.

3. Ibid., p. 94.

Chapter 7:

1. Carl Jung et al, *Man and His Symbols* (New York: Dell Publishing, 1964):p. 48]

Chapter 8: Indirect Emotional Therapies

1. Eleven PM News, WHSV–TV, Harrisonburg, VA (January 17, 1991).

2. *Harvard Mental Health Letter* (October 1992): p. 4.

3. Seneca, *Letters From A Stoic* LXXXVIII, 18, trans. Robin Campbell (London: Penguin, 1969): p. 156.

4. Ibid., XCI, 21, p. 183.

5. Ibid., LXXVIII, 2, p. 134.

6. Ibid., XLVIII, 7, p. 97.

7. Ibid., LXXXVIII, 37, p. 160.

8. Ibid., LXXXII, 9, pp. 142; 24, pp. 143–144.

9. Ibid., CXXII,12, p. 230.

10. Ibid., XCI, 21, p. 183.

11. Carl R. Rogers, *On Becoming A Person* (Boston: Houghton Mifflin, 1961): p. 374.

12. See studies done by Aaron Katcher, M.D., of the University of Pennsylvania.

13. Seneca, op. cit., XV, 7, p .61.

14. *M* Magazine (January 1992): p. 63.

15. Joseph Alsop, *I've Seen The Best of It: Memoirs* (New York: W. W. Norton, 1992): p. 316.

16. Frank Miller, "Joseph Alsop: A Good Great Man," *The Washington Post* (January 31, 1982): p. D-7.

17. Rogers, op. cit., p. 122.

18. James, op. cit., p. 520.

19. Dhammapada I, 1 and 2, quoted in William Hart, *The Art of Living: Vipassana Meditation, as Taught by S. N. Goenka* (San Francisco: Harper, 1987): p. 37.

20. See especially Alfred Ayer, *Language, Truth, and Logic* (New York: Dover, 1952).

21. See especially Alfred Korzybski, *Science and Sanity* (Lancaster, PA: Lancaster Press, 1933).

22. Ellis and Harper, op. cit., p. 69.

23. Ibid., p. 51.

24. Ibid., p. 125.

25. Ibid., p. 203.

26. David Burns, *Feeling Good* (New York: Signet, 1980): p. 326.

27. Ibid., p. 69.

28. Ibid., p. 288.

29. Albert Ellis, *How To Stubbornly Refuse To Make Yourself Miserable About Anything—Yes Anything* (New York: Lyle Stuart, 1990): p. 175.

30. Burns, op. cit., p. 216.

31. Christopher Evans, *Understanding Yourself* (New York: Signet, 1977): p. 290.

32. *Executive Health Report* 21, no. 3 (November 27, 1984): Sec. 2, p. 3, quoting William James in *Varieties of Religious Experience.*

33. *Yoga Journal* (Sept–Oct 1989): p. 107.

34. James, op. cit., p. 269, quoting Henry David Thoreau, *Walden,* (Riverside Edition, abridged): p. 206.

35. Hart, op. cit., p. 114.

36. Ibid., p. 136.

Chapter 9: Direct Therapies

1. Rogers, op. cit., p. 167.

2. James, op. cit., p. 267.

3. *Foundation for Community Encouragement Newsletter* 6, no. 2 (Summer 1990).

4. Ann Landers, *The Washington Post* (December 27, 1991): p. C-4.

5. Alsop, op. cit., p. 60.

6. Ann Landers, *The Washington Post* (April 15, 1977): p. D-2.

7. James, op. cit., p. 198.

8. Bernard Gavzer, "What Keeps Me Alive," *Parade Magazine* (January 31, 1993): p. 7.

9. In a remark to this author.

10. Marjorie Rosen, "Screen," *People Magazine* 36, no. 8 (September 2, 1991): p. 54.

11. Ibid.

12. Viktor Frankl, op. cit.,p. 161.

13. Colman McCarthy, "The Talking Wounded," *The Washington Post* (October 6, 1990): p. A-19.

14. "Did He Kill the Peace?" *The Washington Post* (March 6, 1994) p. C-1.

15. Evan Thomas, "April 19, 1993: The FBI seige and burning of the Branch Davidian compound in Waco, Texas, has been a rally cry for extremist groups," *Newsweek* 125, no. 18 (May 1, 1995): p. 35.

16. Andrea Dworkin, *Mercy: A Novel* (New York: Four Walls Eight Windows, 1991).

17. Ann Landers, *The Washington Post* (June 25, 1992): p. C-8.

Chapter 10: Integrating the Two

1 Ann Landers, *The Washington Post* (September 21, 1994,) p. C-10.

2. Tim Edwards, "Paths to Sobriety," *Newsweek* 118, no. 6 (August 5, 1991): p. 13.

3. Joshua Halberstam, *Everyday Ethics* (New York: Penguin USA, 1993): p. 191.

4. Don Oldenburg, "Making Over the Inner You," *The Washington Post* (March 11, 1992): p. B-5.

5. Karen Horney, *Neurosis and Human Growth* (New York: W. W. Norton, 1950): p. 82.

6. P. Steinfels, "Beliefs," *The New York Times* (August 18, 1990): p. 10.

7. Ellis and Harper, op. cit., pp. 208–209.

8. Nozick, op. cit., p. 113.

9. James, op. cit., p. 128, quoting Spinoza's *Tract On God, Man, and Happiness*, Book ii, Chapter X.

10. Ann Landers, *The Washington Post* (November 24, 1994) p. F-11.

11. James, op. cit., pp. 122–123.

Bibliography

BOOKS

Alsop, Joseph. *I've Seen The Best of It: Memoirs.* New York: W. W. Norton, 1992.

Ayer, Alfred. *Language, Truth, and Logic.* New York: Dover, 1952.

Beattie, Melody. *Codependent No More.* New York: Harper & Row, 1987.

Burns, David. *Feeling Good.* New York: Signet, 1980.

Dworkin, Andrea. *Mercy: A Novel.* New York: Four Walls Eight Windows, 1991.

Ellis, Albert. *How To Stubbornly Refuse To Make Yourself Miserable About Anything—Yes Anything.* New York: Lyle Stuart, 1990.

Ellis, Albert and Robert Harper. *Guide to Rational Living.* North Hollywood, Cal.: Wilshire, 1974.

Evans, Christopher. *Understanding Yourself.* New York: Signet, 1977.

Frankl, Viktor. *The Doctor and the Soul.* New York: Vintage, 1986.

Halberstam, Joshua. *Everyday Ethics.* New York: Penguin USA, 1993.

Hart, William. *The Art of Living: Vipassana Meditation, as Taught by S. N. Goenka.* San Francisco: Harper, 1987.

Horney, Karen. *Neurosis and Human Growth.* New York: W. W. Norton, 1950.

———.*Our Inner Conflicts.* New York: W.W. Norton, 1945.

Izard, Carroll E. *The Face of Emotion* New York: Plenum Press, 1971

———. *The Psychology of Emotions.* New York: Plenum Press, 1991.

James, William. *The Varieties of Religious Experience.* New York: Penguin, 1982.

Korzybski, Alfred. *Science and Sanity.* Lancaster, Penn.: Lancaster Press, 1933.

LeDoux, Joseph. *The Emotional Brain: The Mysterious Underpinnings of Emotional Life.* New York: Simon & Schuster, 1996

Nozick, Robert. *The Examined Life.* New York: Touchstone Books, 1989.

Rogers, Carl R. *On Becoming A Person.* Boston: Houghton Mifflin, 1961.

Seneca. *Letters From A Stoic,* LXXXVIII, 18. Trans. Robin Campbell. London: Penguin, 1969.

Tomkins, Silvan. *Affect, Imagery, Consciousness.* New York: Springer, 1962

Tomkins, Silvan, and Carroll Izard. *Affect, Cognition & Personality.* New York: Springer, 1965.

Uttal, William R. *The Psychobiology of Mind.* Hilldale, N.J.: Lawrence Erlbaum Associates, 1978.

Viscott, David. *The Language of Feelings.* New York: Pocket Books, 1990.

REFERENCE MATERIALS

Merriam-Webster's Collegiate Dictionary. New York: Merriam Webster, 1995.

Roget's Thesaurus. 5th Edition, edited by Robert Chapman. New York: HarperCollins, 1992.

PERIODICALS

Achenbach, Joel. "Drink No Wine After Its Time?" *The Washington Post* (July 24, 1992): p. D-5.

American Health (June 1988).

Blakeslee, Sandra. "Scientist at Work : Joseph LeDoux; Using Rats to Trace Anatomy of Fear, Biology of Evolution." *The New York Times* (November 5, 1996): p. C-1.

Catroux, Betty. *W* Magazine, 22, no. 19 (Fall 1993): p. 58.

Conconi, Chuck. "Personalities." *The Washington Post* (December 11, 1986): p. B-3.

Diamond, Jared. Review of *Naturalist*, by Edward O. Wilson. *The New York Review of Books* (January 12, 1995): p. 18.

"Did He Kill the Peace?" *The Washington Post*, (March 6, 1994) p. C-1.

Edwards, Tim. "Paths to Sobriety." *Newsweek* 118, no. 6, (August 5, 1991): p. 13.

Executive Health Report 21, no. 3 (November 27, 1984): Sec. 2, p. 3.

Forbes Magazine (August 29, 1994).

Foundation for Community Encouragement Newsletter 6, no. 2 (Summer 1990).

Frankel, Glenn. "After the Ordeal, Together Again." *The Washington Post* (September 27, 1991): p. B-2.

Gavzer, Bernard. "What Keeps Me Alive." *Parade* Magazine (January 31, 1993): p. 7.

Goleman, Daniel. "Severe Trauma May Damage the Brain as Well as the Psyche," *The New York Times* (August 1, 1995): p. C-3.

Harvard Mental Health Letter (October 1992, March 1993).

Howard, Johnette. "Jansen's Last Moment is Golden." *The Washington Post* (February 19, 1994): p. A-16.

Jones, Steve. Review of *How The Mind Works* by Steven Pinker. *The New York Review of Books* (November 6, 1997): p. 13.

Landers, Ann. *The Washington Post* (April 15, 1977; December 27, 1991; June 25, 1992: September 21, 1994; November 24, 1994).

M Magazine (January 1992): p. 63.

McCarthy, Colman. "The Talking Wounded." *The Washington Post* (October 6, 1990): p. A-19.

Miller, Frank. "Joseph Alsop: A Good Great Man." *The Washington Post* (January 31, 1982): p. D-7.

Oldenburg, Don. "Making Over the Inner You." *The Washington Post* (March 11, 1992): p. B-5.

Psychological Review 99 (1992): pp. 561–65; 100 (1992): pp. 68–90.

Rosen, Marjorie. "Screen." *People* Magazine 36, no. 8 (September 2, 1991): p. 54..

Schwartz, John. "Putting A Certain Face on Emotions." *The Washington Post* (November 8, 1993): p. A-3.

Seligson, Tom. "We're All Given a Choice." *Parade* Magazine (March 17, 1991): p. 11.

Steinfels, P. "Beliefs." *The New York Times* (August 18, 1990): p. 10.

Sullivan, Kevin. "At 'Studs' Search, A Different Breed." *The Washington Post* (November 14, 1992): p. D-8.

Thomas, Evan. "April 19, 1993: The FBI Siege and Burning of the Branch Davidian Compound in Waco, Texas." *Newsweek* 125, no. 18 (May 1, 1995): p. 35.

"The Wit & Wisdom of the Maestro." *Newsweek* 112, no. 10 (September 5, 1988): p. 55.

Yoga Journal, (September–October 1989): p. 107.

NEWS

Eleven PM News, WHSV–TV, Harrisonburg, Va., January 17, 1991.

Index

Psychological disorders.
  See Emotional disorders
Psychology, cognitive 61

Q

Quasi-determinism and
  emotions 39

R

Racism 105
Rational-emotive therapy 78–80
Reinforcing negative emotions
  103
Rogers, Carl 76, 92, 93
Roosevelt, Franklin D. 76, 96
Russell, Bertrand 78

S

Sadness
  See also Fourth emotion
  and survival 9
  as one of the five basic
    emotions 7, 8
St. Augustine 20
St. Paul 98
Second emotion 11, 58.
  See also Fear
  stance on the fifth emotion 30
Self-consciousness 20
Seneca 71–73, 74
Sense experience.
  See Emperical reasoning
Sensory deprivation 72
Shame 14
Stevenson, Charles 83
Stress, and the fifth
    emotion 27, 28
Substitution, of one emotion
    for another 44, 103–104
Surrender and sadness 8
Swami Ajaya 88

T

Tables & graphs
  emotional therapies
    direct 109
    indirect 108
  emotional value judgments,
    secondary 51, 108
  emotional value judgments:
    actions 53, 54
    primary 50
  the five emotions 11, 58
  the five emotions and four
    mental processes 59
Taking and desire 8
Thatcher, Margaret 31
Therapies
  cognitive 80–82
  community building 93
  connection to group
    by common cause 97–99
    caveats 102–107
    united by an ongoing
      purpose 95–97
    whose goal transcends
      the individual 99
    whose sole purpose is
      support 93–95
  connection to one
    person 92–93
  direct 91–107, 109
  emotionally based 91
  and empirical reasoning 70
  evaluation of 110–114
  including physical activity
    100–102
  indirect 65–90, 108
  integrating approaches
    108–121
  intuitive 84–90
  rational-emotive 78–80
  receptivity to 112
  using both logic and
    empiricaism 77
  utilization 69